A

PRACTICAL

COMPANION

TO

ETHICS

A

PRACTICAL

COMPANION

TO

ETHICS

SECOND EDITION

Anthony Weston

New York   Oxford
OXFORD UNIVERSITY PRESS
2002

Oxford University Press

Oxford   New York
Athens   Auckland   Bangkok   Bogotá   Buenos Aires   Calcutta
Cape Town   Chennai   Dar es Salaam   Delhi   Florence   Hong Kong   Istanbul
Karachi   Kuala Lumpur   Madrid   Melbourne   Mexico City   Mumbai   Nairobi
Paris   São Paulo   Shanghai   Singapore   Taipei   Tokyo   Toronto   Warsaw

and associated companies in
Berlin   Ibadan

Copyright © 2002 by Oxford University Press, Inc.

Published by Oxford University Press, Inc.
198 Madison Avenue, New York, New York 10016
http://www.oup-usa.org

Oxford is a registered trademark of Oxford University Press

Library of Congress Cataloging-in-Publication Data
Weston, Anthony, 1954–
A practical companion to ethics / Anthony Weston.—2nd ed.
p.   cm.
Includes bibliographical references and index.
ISBN 0-19-514199-7 (alk. paper)
1. Ethics.   I. Title.
BJ1025.W43   2001
170—dc21   00-067093

9 8 7 6 5 4 3 2 1

Printed in the United States of America
on acid-free paper

CONTENTS

PREFACE

The first edition of this little book turned out to be the fore-runner of a much bigger project, the full-scale ethics textbook that has now appeared as *A 21st Century Ethical Toolbox* (Oxford University Press, 2001). I therefore come back to *A Practical Companion to Ethics* against a changed back-ground. *Toolbox* works out certain themes in much more de-tail, reducing the weight this book must carry and also im-proving my approach to some of them. *Companion's* Chapter 4, in particular, has been expanded and greatly reworked, as have parts of Chapters 1 and 3. Upon the request of many users, I have added short sections of exercises and applica-tions—"For Practice and Thinking"—between text and notes in each chapter, as well as a few small boxes defining key terms or reviewing key strategies, and sometimes short dia-logues for illustration or practice. The teacher's notes from the first edition have been integrated into the student-oriented exercises or into each chapter's notes. Interested teachers can find more detailed suggestions and examples in *Toolbox* and its extensive teacher's appendix.

The overall aim of this book remains unchanged: to offer an accessible and brief survey of the skills and attitudes that make ethics *work*—and could help it work better—in real-world practice. It is meant to be a different kind of supplementary book for the college ethics course, complementing the theoretical considerations that often consume such courses. It remains resolutely practical, brief, and upbeat. Elaborations and defenses of the more philosophically controversial points are left to other venues. Interested or provoked readers might consult my book *Toward Better Problems* (Temple University Press, 1992) for more fully developed philosophical accounts.

Peter Williams, Tom Birch, Nim Batchelor, and Scott Yost stand out for special thanks among the many friends and colleagues who contributed advice and encouragement to this project. Donald Becker, Earl Conee, Peter Markie, and several other philosophers served as publisher's reviewers for the first edition of this book. David Boersma, David Detmer, Verna Gehring, and Ben Mulvey served in the same capacity for the second. I heartily welcome all readers' comments, criticisms, and suggestions.

A.W.
<weston@elon.edu>

INTRODUCTION

This book is an invitation to ethics. It is meant to fill the gap between the theoretical issues common in the ethics of philosophers and the practical questions of the doubter and the newcomer. One question is: who even *needs* ethics? Another is: why think for yourself? These are real questions, and they need to be answered before the rest of ethics—its theories and its methods and its history—can speak to us.

This book also aims to bring out the connections between ethics and certain useful methods in practical thinking generally. For example, there is a large literature on creative problem-solving: on multiplying options and reframing problems so that the original problem is transformed. There is an equally large literature on conflict resolution and compromise, crucial skills if we are to avoid polarizing values and the people who hold them. This book brings all of these skills into the spotlight.

Finally, this book is concerned with the heart. Too often I have seen students come away from an ethics course knowing a lot about the theories of ethics and how to apply them in specific cases, but with little sense of the deeper call to responsiveness and care that underlies these formalities. In fact, responsiveness and care are crucial. Some of the most intriguing developments in contemporary ethics begin right here: we could think of the new ethical awareness of other animals, for example, as nothing less than an experiment in open-heartedness.

This, then, is a *practical* companion to ethics. It is meant as an essential supplement to the usual first presentation of ethics, and an essential skill-book as one goes on in ethical practice. It invites, explains, improves, expands. It places ethics against a larger practical background, in order to clarify its role and its potential. It aims to uncover creative possibilities where we now seem to have only dilemmas and intractable conflicts. It seeks to open both our minds and our hearts.

It may seem odd that such book is necessary at all. Why can't the great theories of ethics, or the many textbooks and collected readings in ethics, explain ethics well enough by themselves?

The answer is complex—also controversial—and not something we can expand upon here. I will say only this. A better *invitation* to ethics is necessary because most of the main works in ethics tend to take the need for ethics for granted. This is not exactly an objection—the main works in auto mechanics and dance theory take the need for auto mechanics and dance theory for granted too—but it does leave gaps. A supplement can help. Otherwise ethics may seem too academic, or too much trouble. Why think for yourself, and invite social disapproval and uncertainty, when you can just take the word of the dominant authority figures? Why think at all, when we can just act out our feelings? Really, why?

Standard ethics books also seldom discuss the "how-tos" of ethics: how to frame a problem so that it can be most effectively solved; or how to deal effectively, interpersonally or politically, with fundamental ethical disagreements; or why and how feelings matter. Many philosophers prefer to concentrate on ethics' unique intellectual challenges. But most people come to ethics to learn how to *live*. This is a far broader question. And in truth it poses a rich mix of challenges too, to the imagination and to the heart as well as to the head. By concentrating on certain intellectual challenges unique to ethics, we may slight the practical (and creative, and imaginative) skills that are vital to ethics but *not* unique to it. So part of the aim of this book is to rejoin ethics to life skills—to put ethics into its rightful place.

This book therefore does not duplicate the many histories and applications of ethics already available. It hardly mentions the usual theories and their advantages and defects and applications—that's for elsewhere. Once again: this book is intended instead to offer some practical orientation and problem-solving skills, to open up some creative space within the usual formalities, and to give them a heart.

Some of the advice offered in this book may seem obvious. If it does, just remember that we are much better at giving advice to others than at recognizing when we need it ourselves. Actually, we need the advice too, sometimes even the simplest advice. We need the reminders. Moreover, even when a mistake is "obvious," how to carry on in a better way—how to avoid the mistake next time around—may not be obvious at all. It may take some time and care to develop the necessary skills. Give them the time and the care that they need. They will repay your efforts many times over!

A
PRACTICAL
COMPANION
TO
ETHICS

1

GETTING STARTED

~

WHO NEEDS ETHICS?

Why isn't it enough to follow our feelings, or "fly by instinct," when we are thinking about what we should do or how we should live?

Feelings are essential, of course. A life without love, excitement, and even pain is no life at all. No liveable ethic denies this. But feelings are not the whole story. They may be the beginning, but they are not the end. A certain kind of *thinking* must also be part of the story.

Take prejudice. To be prejudiced is to have a strong negative feeling about someone who is of a different ethnicity or gender or age or social class (or . . .) from yourself. If ethics were just a matter of feelings, there ~~~~~~ ~othing to say against such prejudices. It would be perfectly moral to discriminate against people you don't like.

Instinct says yes. Ethics says no. Ethics instead may challenge these very feelings. "Prejudice" literally means "prejudgment": it is one way of not really paying attention. But we *need* to pay attention. We need to ask why we feel as we do, whether our beliefs and feelings are true or fair, how *we* would feel in the other person's shoes, and so on. In short, we need to ask whether our feelings are *justified,* and, when not, what alternative feelings ought to take their place.

So ethics asks us to think carefully, even about feelings that may be very strong. Ethics asks us to live *mindfully:* to take some care about how we act and even about how we feel.

Consider another contrast with "flying by instinct." Instincts and feelings may oversimplify complex situations. We want things to feel clear-cut even when they are not, and so we may persuade ourselves that they are. Mindful thinking, by contrast, is more patient. Where things are really unclear, in particular, feeling may even have to wait. Premature clarity is worse than confusion. We may have to live with some questions a long time before we can decide how we ought to feel about them.

Our feelings are also easily manipulated. For instance, it is easy to be swayed either way by "loaded language," language that plays upon our emotional reactions. Define abortion as "baby-killing," and you create a negative feeling that closes the case against abortion before it really can even be opened. But a "fetus" is not a "baby" (look the words up). On the other hand, if you describe abortion as simply "minor surgery," you suggest that it is both unintrusive and even healthy. It isn't. Either way, we are led into a prepackaged emotional commitment without ever thinking it through. Habit and conformity take over.

Mindful thinking, by contrast, is more complex and open-ended. It is in this spirit that ethics approaches controversial issues of the day, like abortion or professional ethics or the status of other animals. We do care for other animals, for instance. But we also use many of them for food, shoes, chemical tests, even as objects of sport. Should all of this stop? No? Well, should *any* of it stop? Probably. So what kinds of use of other animals should stop and what kinds should not? Why? How do you decide?

These questions cannot be adequately answered by just consulting your feelings. There are too many different possibilities, too many different "uses," too many different opinions and prejudices (on all sides) that need to be carefully sorted

---

A FEW KEY TERMS

What *is* "ethics," anyway? Philosophers and dictionaries often say something like this: ethics is *the study of moral values;* it considers *how best to think about moral values and how best to clarify, prioritize, and integrate them.*

This definition in turn draws on several others. What is a "value," for one thing? In this book, by "values" I will mean *those things we care about; those things that matter to us; those goals or ideals we aspire to and measure ourselves or others or our society by.*

When we speak of "moral" values, we are concerned with a specific kind of values: *those values that give voice to the needs and legitimate expectations of others as well as ourselves.* "Legitimate expectations" may be of many sorts: we rightly expect to be treated with respect, for instance, and with honesty and care.

We often use the terms "ethics" and "morals" interchangeably. Still, it's often helpful to distinguish the moral values we happen to hold from the deliberate process of thinking them through, criticizing, and revising them. The term "ethics" has a more critical, self-conscious edge. Here we try to go beyond *living out* our values to *thinking them through.*

out. Again, it takes some time and care. Maybe even some degree of compromise.

Every moral issue discussed in this book is another example. I will try to suggest that much more intelligent and creative thinking is possible about these issues than we usually suspect. But the key word is "thinking." Ethics invites us to try.

THE DOGMATIST AND THE RATIONALIZER

Thinking is hard, though, and sometimes unpleasant. We may actually have to change our minds! As a result we have developed some pretty effective ways to avoid it. To get started in ethics we need to be warned against some of them.

Why Listen?

We all know the kind of people who are so committed to their moral beliefs that they cannot see any other side, and cannot defend their own beliefs beyond simply asserting and reasserting them—more and more loudly, probably. This is dogmatism. They may appear to listen (or not), but they *will not* change their minds. Name "their" issue (or perhaps *any* issue), and they know the answer already.

To be clear: being committed to a certain set of values—living up to them, or trying to, and sticking up for them when we can—is a fine thing. And there are certain basic moral values that we all share that we are and *should be* deeply and unshakeably committed to. Dogmatism is a problem because some people go much farther. They make no distinction between the basic "givens" of our moral life and everyday moral opinions that are not at all so clear-cut. Every one of their value judgments, to them, has the same status as the Ten Commandments.

Dogmatists tend to disagree about the actual issues, which in fact is a bit ironic. Dogmatists do agree, though, that careful and open-ended thinking about moral issues is not necessary. After all, if you already know the answer, there is no need to think about it. If you need to argue for your position, you admit that it needs defending, which is to say that people can legitimately have doubts. But that can't be true: you already know that your position is the only right one. Therefore, any reasoned argument for your position is unnecessary. And any reasoned argument *against* your position is obviously absurd. So, why listen?

Ethics, once again, paints a different picture. Despite the stereotypes, the point of ethics is generally not to moralize or to dictate what is to be done. The real point of ethics is to offer some tools, and some possible directions, for thinking about difficult matters, recognizing from the start—as the very *rationale* for ethics, in fact—that the world is seldom so simple or clear-cut. Struggle and uncertainty *are* part of ethics, as they are part of life.

It pays to adjust our language as well. Instead of categorical statements of dogmatic opinions, like bumpersticker-style slogans ("Meat is murder," "God is Pro-Life," etc., etc.), we need to try to speak in a way that is less categorical and final. Very few reasonable moral positions can be shoe-horned into a bumpersticker or slogan, clever as they might be. Besides, this way of putting things polarizes views and makes the other side seem stupid and misled. Don't call names either ("You animal-rights fanatics . . ."; "You Bible-thumpers . . ."). Avoid the easy labels ("Liberal," "Right-wing," . . .).

Speaking in a more open-ended way may help you begin to *think* in a more open-ended way too. At the very least it will create quite different conversations! Typically one dogmatic statement just provokes an equal and opposite dogmatic statement. Speak differently and not only your mind but your discussions may open up differently, and more constructively too.

Offhand Self-Justification

I offer some view in a moral discussion. Someone challenges me. My natural first reaction is to defend whatever it was I just said, even if the challenge is exactly on target.

Call this "offhand self-justification." It is a kind of automatic excuse-making or defensiveness, or what we sometimes call "rationalizing." I may not even get to the point of asking if the challenge actually is on target. Indeed, that's the idea. I'd rather not. Self-defense is all that counts. I try to paper over my uncertainties (or insecurities, or half-knowledge, or wishful thinking) by grabbing for some excuse, and any excuse will do. "It's OK to cheat the phone company, because . . . because, well, everyone else does it too . . . because the phone company cheats *you* . . . because . . . ."

Asked for your reasons, you should give them. There is nothing wrong with trying to defend your view. The problem lies with the offhand or automatic spirit (or, more accurately, spiritlessness) of the defense. Once again, it becomes an excuse for not really *thinking*.

> S: Of course the death penalty deters murderers. It's a proven fact that murder rates are lower in states with the death penalty.
> A: I'm not so sure about that. My understanding is that most states with the death penalty have *higher* murder rates.
> S: Well, you can prove anything with numbers.

S initially appeals to "numbers"—comparative murder rates—to support her position. Challenged, though, she does not reconsider her position or explore other possibilities. She just dismisses any studies that disagree with what she believes, and in the process manages to dismiss the very "numbers" she herself just cited. But she doesn't notice. You can tell that in the next discussion she'll be right back citing the same "proven fact."

There are no surefire ways to avoid rationalizing. It takes a kind of self-confidence, honesty, and maturity, which develop slowly. Even then we seldom escape the temptation entirely. Sometimes it's hard to recognize an offhand self-justification when it is right in front of our eyes. Yet there are some useful strategies for overcoming the urge.

Keep in mind how self-defeating it is. When we make excuses to protect behaviors or opinions that really ought to be questioned and changed, we usually end up having to defend our excuses too. In this way we saddle ourselves with *more and more* unintelligent opinions—new ones invented, off the top of the head, to patch up the holes in the old ones. But the new ones are likely to be full of holes too. It's not a winning game.

Watch yourself. Step a little more slowly the next time you find yourself casting about for some excuse to put questions to rest. Ask instead whether you really are justified in the first place.

Watch for that telltale anger or irritation at being challenged. We often find ourselves becoming irritated or angry when our especially precious excuses are too persistently or effectively challenged. But of course, we get angry at the person challenging us, rather than considering that we might really be at fault for offering an offhand excuse in the first place. Better take the irritation as a warning sign.

Avoid the automatic counterattack. Again, watch yourself. Listening to someone else, are you trying to understand, or just waiting for the person to stop so that you can give your comeback? Are you trying to "win," or to learn? Watch your voice tone: are you conveying ridicule, irritation? Take a time-out if you need it. Give yourself some space to think.

ETHICS AND DIVERSITY

It's clear, day to day, that moral values vary. I think speeding is morally OK; you don't. Some societies tolerate homeless populations running into the millions; other societies find it shameful to allow even one person to live on the streets. Some cultures condemn sex between unmarried young people; others encourage it.

Recognizing differences like these can lead us to a useful humility. It helps open our minds a little. And it can give us some space, sometimes, to try to figure things out for ourselves. What's right for you may *not* always be right for me.

It is tempting, though, to go much farther. From our differences about moral values some people conclude that there is no way, or no need, to think carefully or critically about values at all. "It's all *relative*," people say. "Mind your own business." Maybe any moral opinion is really as good as the next. "Relativism" in this sense is often considered a threat or challenge to mindfulness in ethics. Is it?

Diversity and Common Values

Maybe not. For one thing, the diversity of values is probably overrated. Sometimes values appear to vary just because we have different beliefs about the facts. Maybe I am not bothered by speeding because I think it is perfectly safe, whereas you don't. But we both value safety in the same way. That's the basic value involved, and one that, in this case, doesn't vary.

How diverse are basic values? It's an open question. Some philosophers claim that ethics itself is framed by agreements about certain *very* basic values: not causing pain to innocent others, for example, or misleading others for your own ends. Every society must promote a certain degree of respect for others' lives and honesty in social and economic relations if it is to survive at all. Other basic values may still be "relative," though, such as the values attached to sex roles—one example of a kind of value that seems to vary a great deal among cultures. The relativity of values, then, may be somewhat partial, and as the values involved become more basic and more essential, they may converge too.

Besides, mostly we deal with people who share many of our values—and then once again thinking has a natural place to start. Maybe you and I cannot argue with, say, cannibals about the ethics of cannibalism. Maybe. But how often do you argue with cannibals? I have never argued with a cannibal, not even once, but I argue constantly with my own children, whose moral habits as well as eating habits also need some improvement. And I *can* argue with them—they are growing into *our* culture, and have some learning to do. Here, where most of our moral argument takes place, there's plenty of basis for going on together.

Diversity and Critical Thinking

Let us also look more carefully at those cases where values really do differ, even at the basic level. It doesn't automatically follow that thinking isn't needed in these cases. For one thing, we may still need to think more critically about our *own* values (the point of the first part of this chapter). There's plenty to learn anyway.

The same goes for our arguments or discussions with others. People disagree about all kinds of things (Is there life on

Mars? Did the butler do it?), but we don't suppose these other disagreements can't be resolved intelligently. In fact, disagreements usually provoke us to *more* critical thinking. Why not in ethics too? The fact that some people are racists, for example, doesn't prove that racism is only wrong "for us." It only proves that people have some learning to do.

Thus, although relativism may appear to be the very model of open-mindedness, it actually can have just the opposite effect. It can *close* our minds instead.

> U: I support the death penalty. I believe that it saves lives because it makes murderers think twice before killing someone. Besides, the Bible says, "An eye for an eye, a tooth for a tooth."
>
> V: I don't agree.
>
> U: Why?
>
> V: I just don't. That's my opinion and it's as good as yours!

Maybe that's a little blatant, but you get the idea. Here relativism slides right into offhand self-justification. V treats it like a magic key to escape any kind of thinking whatsoever. She cannot be bothered to offer any reasons, let alone engage U's.

In fact, all opinions on this and most moral subjects require further thinking. Are U's arguments good ones? What values stand on the other side? What are V's reasons *against* the death penalty? Is the death penalty really a deterrent? Doesn't the Bible also tell us not to kill? Whether values are "relative" or not, there is no way out of some good hard thinking.

Diversity as the Occasion for Ethics

Sometimes, in fact, the very diversity of values creates the *need* for ethics. Certain decisions shape our lives together, and therefore affect all of us. Polluted air, for example, doesn't merely affect the polluters, or people who think pollution is morally unproblematic. All of us have to breathe it. Likewise, if our country joins a war effort or bans genetically modified foods or legalizes assisted suicide, all of us are to some degree affected. Or again:

> D: I oppose legal abortion.
> E: Why don't you just mind your own business? Like the slogan says, if you're against abortion, then don't have one!

But there is more to it than this. If some of us practice abortion and some do not, the result is a society in which abortion is practiced. The rest of us have to stand for it, at least insofar as we have to stand aside. In such matters, we cannot act as though everyone can simply do as they please without anyone else being affected.

The relativist's stock phrase "Mind your own business" is therefore an antisocial response. It not only lets the relativist avoid thinking: it also refuses to acknowledge that on issues like these, however much we differ, we still need to work out some intelligent and respectful way of going on together. These matters—certain basic moral issues—are not just your own business but *everyone's* business.

Some philosophers argue, in fact, that this is the very point of ethics: to help us arrive at certain standards that we all are to live by when all of us are affected by each other's behavior. On this view, ethics is precisely *for* those cases where "Mind your own business!" doesn't work as an approach to a problem—where we need to work things out together, however much we may differ. We still need to stay in touch, keep thinking, and keep talking. *That* is nothing less than ethics itself in practice.

FOR PRACTICE AND THINKING ∿

Some Questions

We have noted some of the ways in which people close their minds, often without even noticing or admitting that that is what is happening. Now consider *yourself*. When do you get dogmatic? About certain issues more than others? Which ones? When do you tend to rationalize? When do you get defensive?

Give yourself some credit too. What are you *good* at hearing? On what topics are you truly open-minded? And why is this?

What events in *your* life do you now see as occasions for moral learning? What did you learn? What made that learning possible?

Hearing the "Other Side"

Name a moral position that you find especially hard to take seriously. Now, as an exercise in open-mindedness, your task is to write or state this position in as neutral a way as possible. You don't have to be effusive, and don't try to be extremely positive—usually it is easier to be overpositive than to state a view carefully. Just try to state the position in a reasonable way. You may have to do some research to get it right. In class, ask a classmate who holds that position to help you out.

Consider also the *reasons* that are typically used to support this view. What are those reasons? What are the best reasons according to *you*—the reasons that would persuade you if any reasons could?

Again, don't argue with the position. Just look for the strongest defense of the position you can find. On the other hand, you don't have to *agree* with this position either—after all, you picked it because you not only disagree with it but find it hard to take seriously. The point is to try to understand it, and in general to try to get a little distance from your own reactions: to create a little more space for open-mindedness.

A Dialogue

Dogmatism, relativism, and various kinds of offhand self-justification are partly conversational or argumentative moves: that is, they occur in dialogue, in the back-and forth of conversation or argument. Sometimes they are also subtle!

Carefully consider the following classroom dialogue and consider where (and why) you think minds are closed or closing. Then try rewriting the dialogue (or writing your own) to illustrate more open-minded exchanges.

F: Fighting racism and sexism used to be easier than it is now. It's harder to see what to do anymore. Affirmative action, for instance— it's just not so clear an answer.

G: I think it's clear. If Martin Luther King, Jr. were alive today, he'd be against affirmative action!

H: Why do you think that? He was *for* it when he was alive, wasn't he?

G: He always spoke up against what was wrong. I believe affirmative action is wrong, so . . .

J: No, it makes sense. This society is still racist and sexist, you know. And if you know someone is going to discount you because you're black or female, a little extra nudge just makes things equal again.

M: Well, you must be the exception that proves the rule. Everybody *I* know is against all those quotas!

L: I don't think they use quotas. They just check for biased patterns of hiring or school admissions over time.

M: And then what? Besides, how do you "check"? You have to use quotas!

L: Computers or something, I don't know.

P: It's discrimination either way. Either the racism or sexism J talked about, or reverse discrimination to correct past discrimination. Who's to say which is worse?

J: Oh give me a break! Colleges and universities already give preferential treatment to the children of alumni, and athletes, and even students from other parts of the country. What's so different about giving some preference on the basis of race or sex?

P: Right! It's all in your head. You're only discriminated against if that's how it feels to you.

NOTES

The view that values essentially reduce to feelings is sometimes called "subjectivism." The term "subjectivism," however, tends to have many different and even incompatible meanings, often depending on whether or not the person using the term agrees with the view being described. For a discussion and critique of various meanings of "subjectivism" in ethics, see the entry "Ethical Subjectivism" in the *Encyclopedia of Philosophy* (Macmillan and Free Press, 1967).

Rationalizing may be one of the deepest of all pitfalls in ethics (and probably in life generally), and deserves a chapter of its own in any fuller treatment. For some psychological background, including some fascinating and unsettling experiments, see David Myers, *Social Psychology* (McGraw-Hill, 1999), Chapters 2–4. For a useful overview of self-deception, see Chapter 19 of Mike Martin's *Everyday Morality* (Wadsworth Publishing Company, 2001).

There are almost as many characterizations of relativism as there are people who write about it. For a survey, see the articles on "Relativism" and "Moral Relativism" in *The Routledge Encyclopedia of Philosophy* (Routledge, 1998). Chapter 2 of James Rachels, *The Elements of Moral Philosophy* (McGraw-Hill, 1999) is a careful and accessible analysis of "the challenge of cultural relativism." On the prospect of common values across cultures, a good place to start is Sissela Bok's book *Common Values* (University of Missouri Press, 1995).

Beware of the temptation to interpret any kind of skepticism about or resistance to moral argument as some form of relativism. Take that common phrase, "Who's to say?," as in, "Who's to say that we should always tell the truth?" or "Who's to say that sex outside of marriage is always wrong?" This can certainly be a troublesome kind of challenge. Often its function is to put an end to a discussion that is just developing a useful critical edge. Many students, and their teachers too, therefore take it to be an assertion of relativism.

Yet it is not so clear that "Who's to say?" is really meant this way in normal use. Sometimes this little phrase may be just a way of resisting an appeal to authority in ethics—quite possibly a reasonable move. People need some space to think for themselves, as Chapter 2 argues, and questioning the moral authority of those who make dogmatic or sweeping pronouncements may be a way to make that space.

In college students I think it has another function too. When you enter college you enter a period of life in which rapid change is likely and a lot of experimentation and self-redirection take place. At the same time you're confronted by many people and institutions who would love to tell you exactly what to think and do. Surely it's natural in that situation to get your guard up. "Let me be!" This isn't relativism, it's just self-defense. In my experience it's the other extreme—dogmatism—that's more likely, and more perilous.

A useful website on many ethical matters is Lawrence Hinman's "Ethics Updates" site at <www.ethics.acusd.edu>. Hinman's site covers a wide range of moral issues, and also offers a guide to other web-based ethics resources and a useful glossary of key terms in ethics. On relativism in particular, select the "Moral Relativism" box for articles and general definitions.

2

THINKING FOR YOURSELF

From the start we look to others for guidance: parents, teachers, role models. As adults, too, we turn to family and friends for advice and help. We look to our religious and philosophical and political traditions as well. This is how we learn many of our values in the first place, and how they change or deepen over time. And this is how it should be.

Still, it is one thing to rely on others, or our traditions, for advice and help—quite another thing to let others, or our traditions, decide *for* us. Ethics asks us to think for ourselves.

APPEALS TO AUTHORITY

There are three common kinds of appeals to authority in ethics. There are appeals to *social norms*—to the authority of other people or of "society" or of tradition. There are appeals to the *orders* or *commands* of leaders or bosses. And there are appeals to *God,* which are, in practice, either appeals to religious authorities and spokespeople or to authoritative texts such as a religion's bible.

In each of these cases we get the message that we have something much stronger than mere advice or help. When we invoke authorities such as these, we have only to obey: Do what's expected. Follow orders. Obey God. Thinking and deciding for ourselves are not required. Indeed, when this attitude is carried to the extreme, we may be specifically required *not* to think or decide for ourselves.

In fact, however, we have a responsibility to think for ourselves. None of the common appeals to authority can take the place of our own careful and open-minded consideration.

Take social norms first. Certainly social norms are often wise. We may find much to respect in them. Still, they are also all too often products of long habits of prejudice, closed-mindedness, even repression—not wise at all. Don't forget that sexism and racism were, and in many ways still are, social norms. Yes, so are politeness and a basic courtesy. But so are a timid conformism and a suspicion of any new ideas. Social norms are a mixed bag: not to be ignored, but certainly not the last word either.

Likewise, the orders of leaders or bosses can be wrong. We know from recent cases of "whistleblowing" on corporate and public-service abuses—illegal pollution, shoddy or lethal products, police corruption, and so on—that abuses do happen, and that there are strong pressures not to make them public: indirect threats and the tugs of group loyalty as well as direct threats and orders to keep quiet. In response to this problem, many organizations are taking steps to protect whistleblowers and to allow them to bring forward their complaints within the organization itself. Corporations themselves acknowledge that their own norms, and even the direct orders of superiors, are not and should not be absolutely binding. The orders of political and military leaders can be wrong too. During the trial of Lieutenant William Calley for war crimes at the Vietnamese village of My Lai in 1968, *The New York Times* reported the testimony of James Dursi, a rifleman in Calley's company:

> Lieutenant Calley and a weeping rifleman named Paul Meadlo . . . pushed the [villagers] into the ditch . . . . "There was an order to shoot by Lieutenant Calley, I can't remember the exact words—it was something like 'Start firing.' Meadlo turned to me and said: 'Shoot, why don't you shoot?' He was crying. I said 'I can't. I won't'. Then Lieutenant Calley and Meadlo pointed their rifles into the ditch and fired. People were diving on top of each other; mothers were trying to protect their children . . ."

Dursi disobeyed a direct order to shoot. Yet he was right. In general, even when we have direct orders to do something, it is still our responsibility to decide whether to follow them. This principle has repeatedly been affirmed in war crimes tribunals. It is not enough to say, "I was just following orders."

Religious Authority

Appeals to religious authority look rather different. In many religions, God is conceived as omniscient and perfectly good, so God—by definition, some would say—cannot be wrong. Therefore, the commandments of such a God are surely compelling: surely better than our own partial knowledge and dubious goodness, necessarily the proper reference point for our moral action. Appeals to God look like a clear-cut case of a compelling argument from authority.

In fact, things are not so clear. There is, of course, the problem that religions differ. One religion's God may say one thing; another religion's, another. This at least implies that appeals to one religion's God cannot settle matters when people of other religions, or no religion, are involved. This is why Church and State are separate in America: we are a people of many religions who meet and live together on common, and therefore neutral, ground.

But there is a still deeper and more fundamental difficulty. Appeals to God, in practice, are in fact appeals to a religious leader who claims to speak for God, or to a religious text that claims to be the true word of God. And this, inevitably, means the reentry of human claims to authority into the picture.

This is quite a different matter. God may be good by definition, but there are no guarantees about anyone else. Established religions may mirror the distorted and backward social norms just mentioned. Despite the heroism of some individual ministers, for instance, white churches were not notably out in front in the civil rights struggle (not notably behind, either, but that's just the point: they reflected their society). Historically, many churches supported slavery. Every religion's bible, meanwhile, is the product of a long history of human translation, editing, argument, even persecution and centuries of war. Scholars believe, for instance, that the first five books of the Christian Old Testament—which also form the Jewish Torah—represent not one voice, but the work of at least three different writers, woven together later by still other writers. Later still they were translated—from Hebrew to Greek, from Greek to Latin to English—and are still read differently by Jews and Christians.

In fact, then, appeals to "the word of God" are inevitably appeals to human interpretations, human arguments, human points of view. These appeals, as we have already seen, cannot

be the last word. They may have much to offer—sometimes
they may even offer us the very best that human tradition *can*
offer—but still, even then, they cannot simply be put in place
of our own judgment.

The Problem of Ambiguity

Another problem with appeals to God's authority, especially
when we appeal to a sacred religious text such as a bible, is
that the texts are often ambiguous. The stories are more complex than we are encouraged to think, and the morals of the
stories much less clear.

Here is one example. Some Christians insist that the Bible
condemns homosexuality. One common scriptural reference
is to the story of the destruction of Sodom:

> The two angels came to Sodom in the evening; and Lot was
> sitting in the gate of Sodom. When Lot saw them, he rose to
> meet them . . . and said, "My lords, turn aside, I pray you, to
> your servant's house, and spend the night, and wash your feet;
> then you may rise up early and go on your way." . . . He urged
> them strongly; so they turned aside to him and entered his
> house; and he made them a feast, and baked unleavened
> bread, and they ate.
>
> But before they lay down, the men of the city, the men of
> Sodom, both young and old, all the people to the last man,
> surrounded the house, and they called to Lot, "Where are the
> men who came to you tonight? Bring them out to us, that we
> may know [i.e. rape] them." Lot went out of the door to the
> men, shut the door after him, and said, "I beg you, my broth-
> ers, do not act so wickedly. . . . Do nothing to these men, for
> they have come under the shelter of my roof. Behold, I have
> two daughters who have not known man; let me bring them
> out to you, and do to them as you please; only do nothing to

these men, for they have come under the shelter of my roof."
But [the crowd] said, "Stand back!" ... Then they pressed hard
against Lot, and drew near to break the door. But [the angels]
put forth their hands and drew Lot into the house to them,
and shut the door. And they struck with blindness the men
who were at the door of the house, so that they wearied themselves groping for the door. (Genesis 19:1-11)

God destroys the city the next day, after helping Lot and his
family to flee.

This story is complicated and confusing. God does destroy
Sodom, so clearly there is something that He means to condemn. But what? The text does not say. The traditional reading is that the true crimes of Sodom are its shocking level of
violence and its extreme disrespect for strangers. The prophets
Isaiah and Ezekiel specifically refer to the sin of Sodom as the
sin of injustice, oppression, and pride. On this view, homosexuality has nothing to do with it.

We might expect that if anything is specifically condemned
in this story, it is rape. After all, rape is what the crowd had
on their minds, and the crowd, along with the city it stands
for, is quickly punished. But here too things are confusing.
Lot, who is presented as the only relatively decent man in
Sodom, actually offers the crowd his own daughters in the
place of his guests. The angels prevent these rapes too from
happening. But God still saves Lot from the destruction of the
rest of the city. Does not Lot's treatment of his own daughters offend God? Is the shelter of his roof for strangers more
important than the shelter of his family for his own children?

We are reminded that this story was written at a time when
some values were very different than they are now: when, for
one thing, women were regarded as a father's or husband's
property, for him to dispose of as he saw fit. Again we see the
intrusion of human prejudice and blindness into what is sup-

posed to be the word of God. Regardless of what the story does or does not condemn, we might have doubts about its true moral authority.

In any case, again, we are left unclear about just what it is that God condemns about Sodom. That it is homosexuality is a major leap—added, we might suspect, by people who *already* oppose homosexuality and are looking to Scripture for support. But in that case we need to hear and evaluate their reasons, not a forced reading of Scripture to make it yield the desired conclusion. Perhaps there are good arguments, but a facile reference to the story of Sodom is not one of them.

A BIBLICAL IDEAL

This is our responsibility: to think for ourselves. Once again, I don't mean that we must never listen to others. Listening to good advice and thinking in new ways are crucial. Religious texts too have long been sources of great inspiration and stimulation: use them. But it is still up to *us* to interpret, ponder, and decide.

It may help to keep in mind another part of the Sodom story—a part very seldom cited in appeals to God's authority, but a part nonetheless, and in fact right next to the episode just quoted. Just before the angels visit Sodom, they visit the patriarch Abraham in his desert tent. As they leave, they declare God's intention to destroy Sodom if the rumors about it are true.

Abraham is troubled by this. He cannot see the justice of killing the innocent along with the wicked. So Abraham, says the Bible, "went before the Lord." He actually took it upon himself to question God!

> Abraham drew near and said: "Wilt thou indeed destroy the righteous with the wicked? Suppose there are fifty righteous within the city; wilt thou then destroy the place and not spare

it for the fifty righteous who are in it? Far be it from thee to do such a thing, to slay the righteous with the wicked, so that the righteous fare as the wicked! Far be that from thee! Shall not the Judge of all the Earth do right?"

And the Lord said, "If I find at Sodom fifty righteous in the city, I will spare the whole place for their sake." Abraham answered, "Behold, I have taken upon myself to speak to the Lord, I who am but dust and ashes. Suppose five of the fifty righteous are lacking. Wilt thou destroy the whole city for lack of five?" And He said, "I will not destroy it if I find forty-five there." Again he spoke to Him, and said, "Suppose forty are found there." He answered, "For the sake of forty I will not do it." Then he said, "Oh let not the Lord be angry, and I will speak. Suppose thirty are found there." He answered, "I will not do it, if I find thirty there." He said, "Behold, I have taken upon myself to speak to the Lord. Suppose twenty are found there." He answered, "For the sake of twenty I will not destroy it."

Then [Abraham] said, "Oh let not the Lord be angry, and I will speak again but this once. Suppose ten are found there." The Lord answered, "For the sake of ten I will not destroy it". And the Lord went His way, when he had finished speaking to Abraham; and Abraham returned to his place. (Genesis 18: 23–33)

What is the Bible telling us here? Surely not that we should simply do what we're told, and accept whatever authority decides to do. Quite the contrary! Abraham, the revered forefather, did not simply obey. He would not accept injustice even when God Himself proposed to do it. He went to God ("I who am but dust and ashes") and complained. He questioned, he challenged. "Shall not the Judge of all the Earth do right?"

Abraham thought for himself. Moreover, he was honored for doing so. God listened and answered. Indeed Lot himself was saved, the Bible says later, because God was "mindful of

Abraham" (*Genesis* 19:29). So the next time someone acts as though it is ours only to obey the dictates of God (according to them), or ours only to obey some other authority— remember Abraham!

THE QUESTION OF RULES

Similar to the appeal to authority is the appeal to rules, or more exactly, the appeal to what are supposed to be hard-and-fast moral rules. Here too we are told that our task is not primarily to think for ourselves, but to obey. Here too, though, what we are told may not be the whole story.

Like the advice and guidance of others, rules—of a sort, anyway—are necessary. Life is too complicated to think everything through from the beginning. We have to rely on rules of thumb: rough and ready provisional guides that allow us to get on, well enough, most of the time. "Better safe than sorry." "Better late than never." "If it's not broken, don't fix it."

Still, these rules are *rough* guides. They have exceptions. Sometimes late is worse than never. Safety may become such an obsession that we may end up safe *and* sorry. We understand that these rules are not meant to take the place of thinking, but only to give thinking a place to start.

Moreover, such rules often conflict. "If it's not broken, don't fix it"—but then again, "An ounce of prevention is worth a pound of cure." Maybe we're "better safe than sorry"—but then again, "nothing ventured, nothing gained." The point, once again, is that rules can't replace thinking. They are useful aids, nothing more.

Ethics too has rules. But in ethics, very often we seem to think that the rules somehow are absolute. As with our appeals to authority, we sometimes imagine that appeals to ethical rules can take the place of thinking for ourselves.

For example, the philosopher Immanuel Kant insisted that lying is wrong under all—absolutely *all*—circumstances. "Tell the truth" was for Kant an absolute rule. According to Kant, even if a murderer, in pursuit of an innocent victim, comes to you and asks you where his intended victim is, you must answer truthfully. Honesty is not merely the best policy, it is supposed to be the *only* ethical policy.

Problems with Rules

Once again, however, things are not so clear. In the first place, ethical rules, like every other kind of rules, have exceptions. Surely Kant was wrong to say that we should never, ever lie. We *should* lie to save an innocent victim. We honor people who sheltered Jews from the Nazis during the 1930s and 1940s in Europe, and people who sheltered fugitive slaves from slaveowners during the era of slavery in America, even though these acts required systematic deception—nothing so slight as a single lie!—sometimes over a period of many years.

Ethical rules, in reality, are more like familiar nonethical rules of thumb, such as "Better safe than sorry." Ethical rules like "Honesty is the best policy" do not tell us what we always must do. They recommend good policies—never claiming that they must be our *only* policies. Honesty is a good idea—usually. But the person who insists on following such rules in every circumstance, without question, is the kind of person Mark Twain once called, "A good man in the worst sense of the term." We still have to decide.

A second problem with ethical rules is that they conflict— once again, just like nonethical rules. *We* must still decide which rule to follow. Jean Valjean, hero of Victor Hugo's *Les Miserables,* was sentenced to hard labor for ten years because he stole a loaf of bread to feed his starving child. Certainly we have a rule that prohibits stealing—it is even one of the Ten Commandments. "Well, then, stealing is always wrong. End of story!" But it is not the end of the story. For Valjean, it is only the beginning (also for Hugo: *Les Miserables* is a very long book!). We also have a rule that commands us to do everything we can for our children, and preserving their lives is certainly one of the most basic things we must do. These two rules conflicted; Jean Valjean had to make a choice.

A third problem afflicts those rules that mostly escape the problems of exceptions and conflicts. The reason that they escape these problems is that they are simply too vague to be useful. The philosopher Jean-Paul Sartre presented the case of a young man in occupied Paris, during the Second World War, who had to decide between staying with his dependent mother in Paris or escaping to England to fight in the war. Commenting on the decision, Sartre wrote:

> Who could help him choose? [The rules that say we should] "be charitable, love your neighbor, take the more rugged path, etc."? But which is the more rugged path? Whom should he love as a [neighbor]? The fighting man or his mother? Which does the greater good, the vague act of fighting in a group, or the concrete one of helping a particular human being to go on living?

Sartre's point is that actual decisions, real cases, are too specific for rules to determine. "[Rules] are vague," he says, "and ... always too broad for the specific and concrete case we are considering." Rules may give us a general orientation, but how to apply them (and, once again, *which* rule to apply) remains up to us. Once again: in the end, *we* decide. Not the rules. Us.

Consider the Golden Rule, "Do unto others as you would

have them do unto you." It is certainly hard to quarrel with
the Golden Rule as a general guide to living. But in a way that
is just the problem. The Golden Rule is, at best, a *general*
guide to living, not a way to make *specific* decisions. To say,
"Do unto others as you would have them do unto you," is really to say: remember that, in the big picture, others are just
as real, just as conscious, just as important as yourself. The rule
only says: always bear that in mind. Good idea! But the rule
does not say anything specific about what we should *do*. (If
a murderer asks you directions, do you tell the truth? Well, if
you were the murderer, you'd want the truth. On the other
hand, if you were the intended victim . . .) Once again, even
with such rules—golden ones, too—you still must think for
yourself.

Choosing Is Inescapable

Whether we admit it or not, we *do* make our own decisions.
We cannot pretend that we are simply obeying some rules (or
authorities) that settle matters—ours only to obey. In truth,
rules have exceptions: you decide when and why. Rules, like
authorities, conflict: we decide what to do, which rule to follow. Rules are vague: we decide how to apply them. "Honesty
is the best policy"—but it is still up to us to decide when (and
how far!) to be honest. "Thou shalt not kill"—but how many
of us are pacifists?

Choosing is inescapable. The only thing we accomplish by
denying our own responsibility is to make it easier for others to manipulate us. The philosopher Bryan Norton relates
how his older brother manipulated rules for years to make
Bryan do the dishes. If Bryan ate first, his brother cited the
rule, "Whoever gets the dishes out has to wash them." If his
brother ate first, the rule was, "Whoever eats last has to wash
up." If your attitude toward rules is "automatic" in this way,

like a trusting child's, you are not likely to question someone else's use of rules, and you may end up being exploited—not necessarily so innocently as poor Bryan. Let me say it one last time: think for yourself!

FOR PRACTICE AND THINKING ∼

Moral Teachers versus Moral Authorities

Many of our values are shaped by our moral teachers, from parents to role models, and we continue to learn from others throughout life: by the quiet example, by explicit challenge, by inspiration. We need to respect and honor those who teach and inspire us. On the other hand, we need to do so without making them into authorities whose word we take just because it is theirs. Their word should carry weight, but it is not the *last* word—that is always ours.

Name two or three people who have had a special influence on your moral values. Explain how they have influenced you, and acknowledge and honor them. Now imagine that you disagree with them about some major moral issue, as perhaps you already have. Explain yourself to them. Let your disagreement remain respectful, but also take the occasion to find your own moral voice. Give your own reasons. Imagine and write an actual dialogue, or describe some cases in which you and they have disagreed, and why.

A Dialogue

Consider the following dialogue.

A: The Bible says homosexuality is wrong! *Leviticus* is explicit at 20:13. "If a man lies with a man as with a woman, it is an abomination." Thus saith the Lord!

B: Say, what's that you're eating there?

A: Ham sandwich. What does that have to do with anything?

B: Look up *Leviticus* 11:7: "You shall not eat the swine; it is unclean to you."

A: Oh come on!

B: You don't think it's in the Bible?

A: It is in the Bible. I just don't see why you're bringing it up.

B: *Leviticus* condemns all sorts of things, you know. I notice you're wearing one of those nice cotton/polyester blends. But *Leviticus* condemns wearing mixed fabrics (19:19). You shaved—but *Leviticus* condemns cutting your beard (19:27). It condemns harvesting your fields right to the edges (19:9–10) . . . I could go on and on.

A: Those are all just historical relics. Like the ancient Hebrews didn't eat shellfish or pork because they would probably get sick from it. We don't need to care about that anymore!

B: That's another one. *Leviticus* says that eating shellfish is an abomination too (11:11–12). Who are you to decide that you don't need to care about that anymore?

A: They had their superstitions. Historical relics, like I said.

B: You don't get it. If you can dismiss some prohibitions—in fact, just about *all* the other ones in this part of *Leviticus*—as relics and superstitions, why not the prohibition against homosexual relations?

A: *You* don't get it. The Bible says homosexuality is wrong! Isn't that true? Yes or no.

B: Yes.

A: So who are you to say it's not wrong?

Who really doesn't get it? How does this exchange relate to the discussions in the text?

NOTES

Appeals to authority have long been a concern of philosophical ethics, going as far back as Plato's *Euthyphro* (available in many editions, in complete editions of Plato's work, and in partial collections such as the Penguin collection *The Last Days of Socrates*). Here Plato carefully analyzes the relation of the good to the gods, and argues that an independent judgment of values is inescapable, even within religious ethics. For a contemporary commentary on and application of Plato's argument, see James Rachels, *The Elements of Moral Philosophy* (McGraw-Hill, 1999), Chapter 4.

The same need for independent judgment—in fact, once again, the absolute unavoidability of independent judgment—is a modern theme too. It is crucial, for example, to existentialism. A thorough and engaging philosophical introduction to this theme in existentialism (and its history back through Nietzsche to Kant and earlier) is Frederick Olafson, *Principles and Persons* (Johns Hopkins University Press, 1967). Joseph Fletcher, in *Situation Ethics* (Westminster Press, 1974), posed an influential challenge to the appeal to rules, especially in religious ethics, where he called it "legalism."

Here is the prophet Ezekiel on the traditional reading of the sin of Sodom: "Behold, this was the guilt of your sister Sodom: she and her daughters had pride, surfeit of food, and prosperous ease, but did not aid the poor and needy" (*Ezekiel* 16:49). On the *Genesis* passage cited in the text, remember that in Biblical Hebrew, "to know" means to have sexual intercourse. *Genesis* 4:1: "And Adam knew Eve his wife, and she conceived and bore Cain . . . ." For follow-up to the discussion of *Leviticus* in the text, see *A 21st Century Ethical Toolbox*, Chapter 2. On God's willingness to be persuaded by human arguments, see also Exodus 32:1–15, where Moses dissuades God from destroying Israel after the incident of the Golden Calf. Here Moses argues with God almost as with an equal. And the Bible explicitly says that, as a result, God "repented of the evil which He thought to do to His people."

Kant's hard-line view of rules can be found in his "On a Supposed Right to Lie from Altruistic Motives," in his *Critique of Practical Reason and Other Writings in Moral Philosophy* (L. W. Beck, ed., University of Chicago Press, 1949). For development of the criticisms made in the text, see Rachels, *Moral Philosophy,* Chapter 9. It appears that even Kant himself later moderated his view: see the section on "Ethical Duties Toward Others: Truthfulness" in his *Lectures on Ethics* (L. Infield, trans., Hackett Publishing Company, 1981). Modern Kantian philosophers also reject the hard line: for discussion of this very case, see Onora Nell, *Acting on Principle* (Columbia University Press, 1975), pp. 133–136.

Dursi's narration of the My Lai massacre is cited in Howard Zinn, *A People's History of the United States* (HarperCollins, 1980), p. 469. The quote from Jean-Paul Sartre is from "Existentialism," in *Existentialism and Human Emotions* (Philosophical Library, 1957), p. 25. Bryan Norton tells on his brother in *Toward Unity Among Environmentalists* (Oxford University Press, 1992), p. 238.

3

CREATIVE PROBLEM-SOLVING IN ETHICS

Many times we feel stuck when confronting a moral problem. Only a few options come to mind, none of them very appealing. In fact, our most immediate association with the word "moral" seems to be the word "dilemma." Moral *dilemmas*. We are supposed to have two and only two choices—or anyway only a *few*—and often neither choice is much good. We can only pick the "lesser of two evils." But, hey, that's life. Or so we're told.

Is it? In all seriousness: is it? How many alleged dilemmas are actually only what logicians call "*false* dilemmas"? How many times, when we seem stuck, do we just need a little more imagination? For one thing, mightn't there be some ready ways of multiplying options: of simply thinking up other possibilities, options we might not have considered? And how about rethinking the problem itself, so that it might be headed off in the future, or transformed into something more easily resolved? How much farther might we be able to go in ethics if we approached it with a little more creativity?

THE NEED FOR INVENTIVENESS IN ETHICS

Consider a famous moral dilemma: the "Heinz dilemma," from the psychologist Lawrence Kohlberg's research on moral development.

> A woman was near death from cancer. One drug might save her, a form of radium that a druggist in the same town had discovered. The druggist was charging $2000, ten times what the drug cost him to make. The sick woman's husband, Heinz, went to everyone he knew to borrow the money, but he could only get together about half of what it cost. He told the druggist that his wife was dying and asked him to sell it cheaper or let him pay later. But the druggist said "no." The husband got desperate and broke into the man's store to steal the drug for his wife. Should the husband have done that? Why?

Kohlberg used dilemmas like this to probe children's moral reasoning. He claimed that most children go through several different, markedly different, stages of moral reasoning. This is a much-debated theory, but that debate is not our concern here. Our question right now is just: is this a true dilemma or a false one? Does Heinz really have *no* options besides stealing the drug or watching his wife die?

I put this question to my ethics classes after they get a little training in creative problem-solving. Can they think of any other options for Heinz? It turns out that they can, easily. Here are some of their ideas.

For one thing, Heinz might offer the druggist something besides money. He may have some skill that the druggist could use: maybe he's a good house painter or piano tuner or a skilled chemist himself. He could barter, trading the use of his skills for the drug.

For another thing, what about public or charitable assistance? Almost every society in which modern medicine is available has developed some way of offering it to people who cannot afford it themselves. Heinz should at least investigate.

Or suppose Heinz called up a newspaper. Nothing like a little bad publicity to change the druggist's mind. Or to help the sick woman gain a few donations. Think of the appeals you see in hardware stores and community groceries, complete with photos, a town rallying to buy an afflicted kid another chance at life. A thousand dollars, all that "Ms. Heinz" needs, is not a lot of money in today's world.

And why is the druggist so inflexible, anyway? Possibly he needs the money to promote or keep on developing his drug. But in that case Heinz could argue that a spectacular cure would be the best promotion of all. Maybe his wife should get it free! Or Heinz could buy *half* the drug with the money he can raise, and then, if it works, ask for the rest to complete the demonstration.

Then again: why we should trust the "miracle drug" in the first place is not clear. New life-saving drugs require extensive testing, which evidently has not happened yet in this case. Where's the Food and Drug Administration when you need it? Maybe the drug is not worth taking even if the sick woman could get it free. Or maybe she should be paid to participate in a drug test!

So: Heinz *does* have alternatives. There are many more possibilities besides stealing the drug or watching his wife die. This is only a partial list, too. I am always delighted by each new group's ability to come up with new options; always there are a few I've not heard before.

I don't mean that there are no moral issues raised by Kohlberg's dilemma. There are. And of course (I add this point for philosophers) *if* one's goal in raising this dilemma is to illustrate the clash of certain ethical theories, or to make certain philosophical points, then it can be altered to foreclose some of the other options. Certainly some situations really *are* dilemmas. My point, however, is that it is a little too easy to accept alleged moral dilemmas without question, as if somehow dilemmas are the only appropriate or natural form for moral problems. Creative thinking is closed out before we even start. Narrow and limited questions leave us, not surprisingly, with narrow and limited answers.

HOW TO EXPAND YOUR OPTIONS

The practical question is *how* to think more creatively. *How* do we multiply options? It turns out that there are a number of very specific suggestions: actual methods for more imaginative thinking, all of them as applicable in ethics as anywhere else.

Breaking "Set"

A little psychology is useful at the start. Our thinking is often limited by habits and unconscious assumptions that have worked well for us in the past. Psychologists use the word "set" to describe these habits and unconscious assumptions. (They're like concrete: at first they're fluid, but they quickly "set," and then we can't move.) "Set" can be so powerful that we literally cannot see any other options, even those right before our eyes.

Understanding "set" helps us appreciate some of the more unusual methods for expanding our options. To break "set" we need to loosen up, try something new, maybe even something that seems peculiar, embarrassing, or improbable. It may feel forced, but that's just the point: we're trying to force our way beyond our own habits.

Here is one method, probably the most obvious, and for that very reason the most commonly overlooked. *Ask around.* Listening to other people is not a bad idea anyway, just to understand them better and broaden your own horizons. Specifically in problem-solving, asking around (asking *anyone* else— friends, children, strangers on the bus, oracles . . .) is an excellent way to get new ideas: to break set. You don't have to follow their advice—but they can certainly give you a fresh perspective.

Brainstorming is another good method. Brainstorming is a process in which a group of people try to generate new ideas. The key rule is: defer criticism. It is tempting and "safe" to react to any new suggestion with criticism. In brainstorming we do just the opposite: we consider how some new idea *could* work, not why it probably won't. Even a crude and obviously unrealistic idea, passed around the room, may evolve into something much more realistic, and meanwhile it may spark other new ideas. Ideas hitchhike on each other. Let it happen.

One further rule often used in brainstorming is that quantity is important. Some groups set quotas for new ideas and allow no criticism at all until the quota is met. This also helps new ideas to percolate and gives people room to think in an exploratory way, free from the fear of being criticized.

If you're still stumped, problem-solving expert Edward De Bono has another, truly wild suggestion. Go to the dictionary, or to any book for that matter. Open it to some page and pick

out a word at random—any word will do. Then see what associations that word suggests. Immediately your thinking has
a truly new stimulus. You are not just going around in the same
old circles. De Bono calls this method *random association.*

Once again it may seem silly. Once again, though, some such
stimulus is just what we need in order to break our "set." We
will still need to work on the new ideas once we've found
them, but random association is a wonderful way of generat-
ing them.

In the face of the Heinz dilemma, for instance, you might
turn to the dictionary for random associations. When I did it,
the first word I found was "oboe." "Oboe?" I said to myself.
"You've got to be kidding!" Then I thought: Well, an oboe is a
musical instrument; an oboe-like instrument is used to charm
cobras in India; maybe Heinz could somehow charm the druggist? How? Well, I'm not sure, but it seems like a good idea for
Heinz at least to talk to the druggist again.

Back to oboes. People play such instruments; people have
skills; Heinz has skills: aha! From here we might begin to think
about bartering skills for the drug. The next word I found was
"leaf." Leaf: "Turn over a new leaf"? "Read leaves"? (Hmm—
foretelling the future, as people used to do with tea leaves?
How do we know that this drug is any good . . . ?) Maybe Ms.
Heinz should use leaves instead of drugs. (Are there herbal
remedies . . . ?). Do you see how thinking begins to loosen up?

The Intermediate Impossible

Yet another possibility: De Bono proposes a method he calls
the *intermediate impossible.* If you have a problem, start by
imagining what would be the perfect solution. Quite probably the perfect solution would be too costly, or physically impossible. But don't stop there—don't just give up and go back
to where you started. Work backward slowly from what's

perfect-but-impossible toward "intermediate" solutions that *are* possible, until you find a possibility that is realistic. In short, make your very first step a big and wild one—otherwise you may never take a big step at all.

Think for example of the problem of speeding—people driving faster than the speed limit, especially to the point that other drivers are endangered. It's both a moral issue and a practical one. And we know the usual option: ticket more speeders. Couldn't there be others?

What would a "perfect" solution be? How about: cars that actually *can't* speed—cars that just don't go that fast. This kind of built-in constraint isn't realistic, I suppose, because people sometimes need to go extra-fast: in emergencies, for instance, or when passing on two-lane roads. But this first and unrealistic idea may lead us to others that might be practical. For example, what about cars that automatically sound a siren or flash lights when they go too fast? Speeding would still be possible, then, but it would also be immediately evident to everyone. You and I would know who to look out for; the police would know who to stop.

Or maybe we could build speed constraints into the roads themselves. Suppose special undulations were designed into road surfaces so that cars begin to vibrate unpleasantly when the speed limit is exceeded. Then roads could enforce their own speed limits!

Also "perfect" would be if people simply didn't want or need to speed in the first place. This suggests at least one good "intermediate" solution: to try to reduce the *pressures* to speed. For instance, some people speed because they are compelled to make it to work at a particular time regardless of traffic or weather or family needs. It might be better to let workers' work day begin whenever they arrive, so that they needn't rush to start at a fixed time. This would give us a lot more flexibility in the rest of our lives as well!

I use the "intermediate impossible" myself for all manner of practical problems: organizing a class, buying a car, negotiating with my children. I know first-hand how it can lead to dramatic and competely unexpected new ideas. It can also move us decisively beyond the tendency to just complain about a problem, or to stick to our side in a fight, without making any progress. When we actually arrive at an idea of what we *want*—not just what we don't want—we sometimes discover that it is not so different from what "the other side" wants. Or not so different from what we've got already.

You see, anyway, how new ideas arise. They are there to be found: the crucial step is to *look*. Confronted with two or three bad choices and the demand to make a decision, start brainstorming. Free-associate. Ask around. Get out your dictionary. Don't let anyone tell you that you have no other options. You can't find out until you start looking for them.

HOW TO REFRAME PROBLEMS

A more radical approach is often possible too. There is a particular kind of set I call "freezing the problem." We freeze a problem when we act as though all we can do is to cope with the problem, accommodate ourselves to it, react after it has happened. Suppose, though, that the problem itself can be changed, made less serious, or even eliminated. The key question might be: what about trying to prevent the problem from even coming up? What about thinking preventively, so that in the end there is no problem left at all?

Some friends of mine loved to have fires in their fireplace. But they lived in a house so designed that when they wanted to use the fireplace, they had to haul firewood through the whole house to get it there. The result was that they seldom built fires, and when they did they made a huge mess. For years they just tried to carry wood more carefully. Later they were proud of themselves for hauling wood in a box, to avoid dropping splinters and dirt all through the house. But this was awkward too. The halls were still small, the box large.

No doubt there were still more creative options: maybe getting wood cut into really tiny pieces, or buying the dirt-free fake logs you see in hardware stores, or getting some nice dirt-colored carpet so the mess was less noticeable. Once again, however, notice that all of these ideas left the problem as it was. They froze the problem rather than changing it. Suppose that instead we ask: Is there a way to prevent this problem from even coming up?

Here is what a precocious cousin finally proposed: knock a hole in the wall right next to the fireplace and put in a little door and a woodbox. My friends were delighted and did just that. Voila—end of problem!

My friends missed an obvious and simple alternative because they were preoccupied with better ways to haul wood through the house. They were becoming very good at accommodating themselves to a badly designed house, when in fact they needed to *change* the house. Odd as it may sound, "solving" problems is not the only way to deal with them! Sometimes it is not even the best way. Notice that my friends did not actually solve the problem of how to haul wood through the house without making a mess. They simply eliminated that problem. Now they don't haul wood through the house at all. There is no problem left to solve.

Preventive Ethics

Faced with a moral problem or "dilemma," then, one fundamental question we need to ask is whether the problem itself can be changed, made less serious, or even eliminated. We need to look at the bigger picture, at the roots and causes of such problematic situations, and ask what we can do about *them*.

Kohlberg has us worry about whether Heinz should steal a drug that is necessary to save his dying wife. Maybe Heinz can find some other way to save his wife or get the drug. But there is a range of more probing background questions that Kohlberg does not ask. Why does the sick woman have no insurance? Why can't public assistance help her? If either insurance or public assistance was a real option, Heinz's dilemma would not come up in the first place.

We have learned to ask what should be done when the family of a person in a "persistent vegetative state" wants her respirator turned off. Now let us learn to ask the background questions, like why nobody knows her wishes on the subject, or why the hospital's lawyers have the last word. Why not mandate much clearer "living wills"—a person's declaration of her desires about what she wishes done should she become comatose, made while she is still of sound mind? Why not take end-state care out of hospitals entirely and back to hospices or even homes, where families have the last word?

Executives and managers worry about whether whistleblowers are being disloyal or destructive, while consumer advocates worry about how to encourage and protect them. But what about the preventive questions? How could the need for whistleblowing be prevented in the first place? Some reformers propose much more effective ways of protecting lines of communication and complaint within corporations and bureaucracies, thereby reducing or eliminating the need to go public with disruptive and controversial accusations, ruining one's own professional life and possibly those of others along the way. Others have suggested more effective public participation in large corporations, so that abuses become less frequent. Some experiments have been tried along these lines. We need to pay more attention. The possibility of such reforms is every bit as much an answer to the problem of whistleblowing as the usual hand-wringing about the conflicting values of loyalty and honesty and such. Why let such conflicts become so intense in the first place?

We worry about "the drug problem." But all we usually see are offenders—dealers and users—and all we usually consider is punishment: jail, mandatory sentencing, more police. Once again a whole range of constructive possibilities is being ignored. There are truly fundamental questions here, like why people are attracted to drugs in the first place, and why it is so difficult to get free later. Surely part of the appeal of drugs, at least initially, is that they offer some excitement in the midst of an otherwise uninteresting life. Then one bottom-line question is: are there less lethal ways to make life more interesting? Yes, obviously. Well, *what* ways?

Now there's a fine question! What can we do to make life so interesting that people are no longer tempted to escape through drugs? A truly "better problem": no longer punitive, widely engaging, promising for all of us.

Of course, problems cannot always be reframed. Sometimes there is no time. Heinz, for example, may have very few options left. A person on a respirator in a hospital is already quite thoroughly "framed." There may be some moral questions that cannot usefully be reframed even if there is time. The point, though, is that we tend to overlook even the *possibility* of reframing our problems. Don't simply assume that reframing is impossible, and resign yourself to just shouldering the same old burdens. Raise your head a little; look around; give yourself some room to move.

"Opportunism"

Albert Einstein once said that every difficulty is also an opportunity. Suppose we take him at his word. Could *moral* problems also be opportunities, rather than simply problems to be solved or even eliminated? Could it be that we can make use of what *seems* to be a problem in some new and unexpected way?

Here's a problem: if you go to any nursing home or assisted-living center, you will find people desperate for something constructive to do. There are some organized games and other activities, but the overall feeling is simply that time is being filled. Professionals are even trained and hired to find ways to keep the residents busy—disguising what we normally assume to be the simple fact that really there *is* nothing for them to do. There is no one even to hear their stories.

You could look at this situation and see only a difficulty: how to fill up elderly people's time. You could also look at the very same situation and see an opportunity. Here, after all, are a large number of experienced people who have certain physical limits but who nonetheless have time, love, and experience to pass on. Couldn't anyone use a little of that?

Of course! What about children, for example? Many parents are desperate for good-quality child care, for a setting in which children can be cared for and can learn and grow into the larger community in richer ways than they might at home. And therefore, right now, in another building possibly quite near the assisted-living center, professionals are once again trained and hired, this time to find ways to keep children busy and maybe even teach them something. And once again we normally assume that there is nothing especially constructive for the children to do either. Just "play", or, in the cheaper day care centers, watch TV.

Mightn't precisely the neediness of *both* groups also have its hidden opportunities? Can't we make one solution out of two problems? Why not bring the very young and the very old *together* in a setting in which both can help each other? The old can tell their stories to the very people who love stories above all. And the young can help tend to the needs of the old, learning something of life cycles and of service in the process. In every traditional society in the world the old are the ones who initiate the young into the life and history and stories of the culture—and the young are not shielded from the fears and losses that the end of life brings. They help out. What they could offer each other!

This idea is what De Bono would call a "raw" idea—the beginning of something truly creative, with the details still to be sorted out. It needs work. Fine. Examples like these give you at least a glimpse of what really might be possible. Even our *problems* have creative possibilities!

PROBLEM-SOLVING STRATEGIES AT A GLANCE

To expand your options:

- Ask around
- Brainstorm (i.e., in a group, generate a set number of ideas *without criticism*)
- Use random or free association
- Seek the "intermediate impossible"

To reframe your problem:

- Think preventively (are there ways to keep the problem from even coming up in the future?)
- Ask: Is the problem also in some way an *opportunity?* (And then: for *what?*)

FOR PRACTICE AND THINKING ~

Problem-Solving Practice

To limber up your creativity, practice the methods in this chapter all the time, not just in ethics. Bored? Challenge yourself to figure out ten, or twenty, new and different uses for some everyday object, like a brick. Yes, it can be a paperweight or a doorstop or a shelf support. What else? Suppose you tape on a return-postage-guaranteed junk mail reply form and drop it in a mailbox—a good way to protest junk mail. Suppose you leave it in your yard until you want to go fishing, and then collect the worms underneath. Suppose . . .

Or again: What can you do with a . . . cheap ballpoint pen (besides write)? . . . a piece of paper? . . . a rotten apple? . . . a bad joke? When you get stuck, use the methods from this chapter!

Now pick some specific practical problems around your school or area and challenge yourself to add to (let's say, triple or quintuple) the number of options usually considered. For practice, they needn't be moral problems. Try problems like waste (styrofoam cups, lights left on all the time, newspaper, etc.); alcoholism and other addictions; too much television; lack of inexpensive travel options; alternatives to on-the-air fund raising for public radio; parking issues at school or elsewhere; or low voter turnout. A look at any newspaper will produce many more. Don't forget to try to *reframe* these problems too. How might you prevent them from even coming up? And what might too much styrofoam or too little parking space be an *opportunity* for?

Moral Problems

Now consider more familiar moral issues, and use the option-multiplying and reframing methods as you just did with the practical problems above. Once again, challenge yourself to triple or quintuple the number of options usually considered.

This will feel awkward at first—it seems not quite serious enough an approach for moral issues, which we're always taught must be serious indeed. Try them anyway. Get used to it: give the methods a chance to show what they can do.

What alternatives might there be for a convicted murderer, for instance, besides capital punishment or life in prison? I expect that you can think of four or five serious options in five minutes if you apply yourself. And while you're at it, what about that seemingly hardest of our current moral issues—abortion? Give that one some real thought: I will tell you in advance that there's a *lot* that can be done with it with even a little creative thinking.

Don't settle for an idea that's only a *little* bit different from the usual. The methods in this chapter can take you farther than that. Get wild!

Go Public

Some brainstorming groups go on local radio stations every week or month to offer call-in group problem-solving sessions. One member writes: "Most callers want to solve their problems, and some have ideas for earlier callers, which is what we want from them. But mostly we inspire some people with our attitude about 'considering the possibilities.'"

Now that you have built up some problem-solving expertise, think about going public as a group yourselves. That is, advertise yourselves as a problem-solving or brainstorming group, and invite people to send in problems—especially moral problems. Set up meetings on campus, or elsewhere. Several people in San Francisco have set up a "salon" called the "Brain Exchange" which holds monthly problem-solving sessions, announced in the papers and in mailings to a six-hundred-person mailing list. They charge five dollars at the door to cover costs. Sometimes they throw a potluck to which everyone brings one dish and one problem. Try it yourself!

NOTES

For more on these and other creative problem-solving methods, see my *A 21st Century Ethical Toolbox*, Chapters 11 and 12. For a general introduction to problem-solving broadly conceived, see Marvin Levine, *Effective Problem-Solving* (Prentice-Hall, 1993) and the many works of Edward de Bono, such as *Lateral Thinking* (Harper and Row, 1970).

As I say in the text, one can certainly redescribe the "Heinz dilemma" or other examples to cut off each new option as it comes up, so that finally Heinz must "just choose." If your purpose is solely to illustrate the clash of different ethical theories, this may seem to be a natural move, and trying to come up with new options may indeed seem to confuse things, even to miss the point. And of course there *are* genuinely hard choices. Nonetheless, there are often other options too. We need the encouragement—more than we usually get in ethics texts—to look for them, to avoid locking ourselves into unpromising problems. From a philosophical point of view, moreover, the possibility of creatively rethinking moral problems raises the question of the very nature of moral problems. If moral problems are like puzzles, distinct and well defined, then it does "miss the point" to try to rethink them creatively. Pragmatic philosophers, though, argue that moral problems are more like large, vague regions of tension, not at all distinct or well defined. "Problematic situations," Dewey called them. No "solution" can really be expected. They are also, for just the same reason, regions of opportunity. Constructively engaging the problem—trying to change it into something more manageable, making something of the opportunities—is the most intelligent response, and often the *only* intelligent response.

For further discussion of these points, and an extended argument for the last claim, see my book *Toward Better Problems* (Temple University Press, 1992). For Dewey's view, see James Gouinlock's collection *The Moral Writings of John Dewey* (Macmillan, 1976). The term "preventive ethics" is Virginia Warren's: see her essay "Feminist Directions in Medical Ethics," *Hypatia 4* (1989) and my discussion in *Toward Better Problems,* pp. vii–viii, 24–28, and 183.

The Heinz dilemma is cited from Lawrence Kohlberg, "Stage and Sequence: The Cognitive-Developmental Approach to Socialization," in D. A. Goslin, ed., *Handbook of Socialization Theory and Research* (Rand McNally, 1969), p. 379. For a critique of Kohlberg's conclusions see Carol Gilligan, *In a Different Voice* (Harvard University Press, 1983), pp. 27-38. There is an extended discussion of the Kohlberg-Gilligan debate in Eva Kittay and Diana Meyers, eds., *Women and Moral Theory* (Rowman and Littlefield, 1986). Astonishingly enough, subjects in Kohlberg's studies were graded as morally "immature" if they started exploring other possible options for Heinz. The researchers concluded that these subjects just didn't understand the dilemma. In fact, I think, they understood it better than the researchers. They understood it as a *false* dilemma, which is exactly what it is.

On whistle blowing, see any recent anthology in business ethics, such as Tom Beauchamp and Norman Bowie, eds., *Ethical Theory and Business* (Prentice-Hall). For questions of "pulling the plug," see any recent bioethics anthology or casebook, such as Thomas Mappes and Jane Zembaty, *Biomedical Ethics* (McGraw-Hill). For an extended discussion of the abortion issue using the tools offered in this and the next chapter, see *Toolbox,* Chapter 17. For general information on the Brain Exchange, see *The Book of Visions* (London: Institute for Social Inventions, 1992), pp. 325-326. For a thousand more new ideas to improve our lives—real creativity at work!—check out the Institute's website at <www.globalideasbank.org>.

4

DON'T POLARIZE—CONNECT

~

Our moral values often diverge. Sometimes they stand in painful opposition. Sometimes they are just imperfectly compatible, or pull in different directions. Either way, divergence can be a practical problem. We need to decide how to go on when we ourselves feel divided, and we need to be able to go on together when our values diverge from those of others. One of the major tasks of ethics is to offer some help doing so.

"RIGHT VERSUS RIGHT"

One problem is that we often exaggerate our divergences, making them much worse than they might be. We *polarize* values.

Look around at the bumperstickers you see on major moral issues. On most of these issues there are usually supposed to be just two, clearly distinct and opposite positions. On abortion,"pro-life" sets itself up against "pro-choice," and vice versa. On gun control, assisted suicide, gay marriage, and a host of other hot issues, it's often just "yes or no." Almost no other options get discussed. *Time* magazine did a famous cover about the standoff between timber interests and endangered spotted owls in the Pacific Northwest: they labeled it "Owl versus Man." Once again: no ambiguity, no gray areas, no middle ground. Sharp, dramatic, bitter—it makes a good headline.

Polarizing values has another side too. We usually suppose that one side—our own, of course!—is completely right and the other side completely wrong. We polarize values in order to picture ourselves as totally justified, totally right, and the other side as totally unjustified and totally wrong. All good on one side, all evil on the other. Day and night, black and white, us and them. Polarizing values therefore makes things crystal clear, protects us from doubts, justifies us completely. Our choices become easy.

But polarizing values is a bad idea. Reality is more complicated, more interesting, and maybe, just maybe, much more promising.

In nearly every serious moral issue, the truth is that both sides have a point. Or rather, *all* sides have a point, since there are often more than two. All sides speak for something worth considering. Each side is right about *something*.

To put it another way: most moral conflicts are real, not just mistakes by one side or the other about what really matters. There is genuine good on *both* sides—on *all* sides. "Only dogmatism," wrote the philosopher John Dewey,"can suppose that serious moral conflict is between something clearly bad and something known to be good, and that uncertainty lies wholly in the will of the one choosing. Most conflicts of importance are conflicts between things which are or have been satisfying, not between good and evil."

Again—they are choices between one good thing and another. Not "right versus wrong" but "right versus *right.*" We need to start by honoring that fact.

PIECES OF THE PUZZLE

Suppose that we try a new tack in approaching moral debates. Instead of asking which side is right, let us ask what *each* side is right *about.* That is, instead of approaching any other view looking for its weak points (according to us), start the other way around. Look for its strong points. Assume that it has some; the challenge is to find them. Even moral arguments that make absolutely no sense to you do make sense to others who are every bit as intelligent and well intentioned as you. There's got to be *something* in them. Figure out what it is.

What Is Each Side Right About?

Take the "assisted suicide" debate. The question is: should doctors be able to assist certain people to enable their own dying—say, people who are approaching death or total disability and are in great pain?

One side says yes: assisted suicide may be the only way in which some people can finally escape their unrelenting pain. Besides, we are free individuals entitled to make that choice.

The other side says no: allowing and perhaps encouraging doctors to kill, or even just to assist in death, takes a step toward devaluing life, and who knows where it will lead. Life is precious even in pain.

This is a difficult matter, for sure. But it is difficult precisely because both sides have valid points. Freedom from pain matters, and autonomy matters, and also respect for life matters. *Both sides are right.*

Most of us can spell out the values on both sides of an issue like this if we give it some thought and take care to avoid oversimplifying the issue. It just takes some exploring, with at least a somewhat open mind. Doing a little research, maybe. Listening, actually *listening,* without worrying about our "comeback," to what people on other sides are saying. Reminding ourselves that they have some pieces of the puzzle too. So do we. But it's very unlikely that any of us have the whole picture all by ourselves.

What Is Each Theory Right About?

Perhaps you already know something about traditional ethical theories or moral systems, or perhaps you are are studying them now. They can help too. Secular ethical theories such as theories of rights, for example, give us a way to express and connect values. It's often a helpful question to ask what specific rights are at stake, on either or both sides, in a problematic moral situation. In the case of assisted suicide, for instance, one right with which we surely have to come to terms is each person's right to make fundamental, life-or-death choices for themselves. That's part of the puzzle too.

Ethical theories or moral systems may also give us unexpected and deeper insight into a problem than we had before. The philosopher Immanuel Kant proposed a striking way to think about suicide. "If [we] kill [ourselves] in order to escape from painful circumstances," he wrote, "we use a person [ourselves] merely as a means to maintain a tolerable condition to the conclusion of life." Once life offers us no more pleasure we conclude that our life has no more value. But this move, so very natural if you think just in terms of pleasures and pains, is for Kant a fundamental mistake. Our lives, he argues, have value *in themselves,* not just as a means to something else, even of our own. We must respect our *own* lives just as we must respect the lives of others around us.

A subtle point—yes. Subtlety is part of what ethical theories have to offer. They can help us to see farther, and to see more, than we could see without them.

Once again, though, it doesn't follow that only one such theory is right. Rather than ask *which* theory is right, we need to ask instead, once again, what *each* theory is right *about.* We're not necessarily stalemated if we can't choose between them—that's only if we assume that we have to finally go with just one. But we don't. Each highlights certain values left to the side by the others. Just like the different "sides" in the popular debate, each has a *part*—but still only a part—of the puzzle.

GOING AHEAD TOGETHER

Probably the chief reason we hesitate to acknowledge right on both (all) sides of a moral debate is that we're afraid that then we'll be unable to do or decide anything. If both sides are right, what can we *do?* How can we possibly resolve the question, move ahead? Won't we then just be stuck?

No. There are many ways of going on from the acknowledgment that both (all) sides have a point. In fact, people who deal regularly with conflict resolution usually insist that only such an acknowledgment makes it *possible* to go on constructively. Moreover, most of the conflict resolvers' methods are familiar. All of them are so eminently sensible that nothing in this section will be a surprise—though I hope it may be an inspiration. The task is to put them to use *in ethics.*

Practical Strategies

Specifically, the task is to *integrate* the values at stake. If both sides (or all sides) are to some extent right, then we need to try to honor what is right in each of them. We need to try to answer to *all* of the important values at stake, rather than just a few.

This is a lot less mysterious than it may sound. In fact, we do something of the sort constantly. Suppose that for our summer vacation my partner wants to go to the beach and I want to go to the mountains. We could just battle it out, or flip a coin, and end up doing one or the other. That's how it goes sometimes—a "win/lose" battle.

A little better would be to compromise, to "split the difference." Maybe this year the beach, next year the mountains. Or maybe we could do a little of each this year. Though compromising is sometimes treated as disgraceful or weak willed, here it seems to be quite the opposite: a clear-headed acknowledgment of the diversity of values at stake, and an attempt to answer at least partly to both of them. Simple.

But perhaps we can do far better. Suppose that she and I try to figure out *why* we want to go to the beach or the mountains. Maybe it turns out that she wants to be able to swim and sunbathe, and I want to be able to hike. These goals are not incompatible at all. There are some great lakes in the mountains, and some great hiking trails near the ocean. Both of us can have exactly, or almost exactly, what we want, and at the same time too.

Or suppose tonight my daughter and I are at home and she wants quiet and I want music. It would be crazy for us both to insist that only *our* desire is "right" and fight it out until one of us gets just what we want. Why not just have music for a while and then quiet? A little of both. Or we can work in different rooms. Or I could get a pair of earphones, in which case we could both have *exactly* what we want. Here we move beyond mere compromise to a truly "win/win" solution. It may turn out that our competing desires aren't incompatible at all.

Moreover, sometimes when we really look into the values on the "other" side, we recognize that some of them are not just compatible with our own but in fact are the *very same* values we hold ourselves. Though we tend to focus on our disagreements, normally there are background agreements that may be far more important. For example, in the vacation question, my partner and I agree from the start that we want to spend our vacation outside, in nature. It may be that the exact location matters much less than simply being outside together, and being physically active. Suppose that we started our negotiation there, on common ground. Basically, once again, we're on the same page. We're in it together. Only the details need to be worked out.

Assisted Suicide

Let us now come back to moral issues to put these strategies to work. Take the assisted suicide debate. Is there a space for the creative integration of values here? I think so.

For starters, both sides agree about something basic: that it is a very bad thing to suffer such pain that death seems appealing by comparison. That is clear and central common ground.

Right away, then, the possibility of reframing the problem suggests itself. What can we do to make the end of life less painful? What about developing super-powerful painkillers? What about removing the barriers that still block some dying people from using massive amounts of morphine or other painkillers that would be addictive or otherwise harmful if used by healthy people?

There's more. It turns out that it is not always the pain that makes people seek assisted suicide. Some of my students found a website that included biographies of the people that Dr Jack Kevorkian—the famous (some say infamous) free-lance crusader for assisted suicide—has helped to die. Though it was a pro-Kevorkian website, the students began to realize that Kevorkian became a last resort for many people because they were not only in pain but also lacked any kind of family or social support. They felt helpless, useless, and abandoned.

Neither side would say that in this kind of case the right "answer" is death. The real answer is to create communities of care such that people are not abandoned in this way. That's a challenge to all of *us,* too, not just to stand by and judge the morality of certain kinds of suicide, but to keep people from the kinds of losses that drive them to such desperation in the first place.

On the other hand, sometimes there *are* people whose pain is so intense and unavoidable that it seems hard to deny that death can be a considered and humane choice. Your heart goes out to them, and I for one know that in their situation I might well wish the same thing.

It's possible that many people on *both* sides would be willing to accept a policy that allowed assisted suicide under tightly controlled conditions. Several independent doctors would have to concur; waiting periods could be required; double and triple checks would be necessary to be sure patients were not just depressed; communities and governments would need to be sure that people in pain always have alternatives—but *then,* given all this, if people still resolutely seek to die, maybe it is time to respect their wishes. It may be possible, in short, to legalize assisted suicide in a limited way that both acknowledges the genuine dangers (fears of freelance "Doctor Deaths," like Kevorkian; dangers that it will become an "easy way out") while also recognizing that, sometimes at least, it can be a humane and proper choice.

You might be interested to know that just this kind of policy has been adopted in Oregon (and recently reaffirmed by 60% of the voters), with results that, while still controversial, at least don't sound like an epidemic of suicides. About twenty-five people have secured permission for medically assisted death each year since the option became available.

"Owl versus Man"

Now consider the so-called "Owl versus Man" debate. Once again the first thing to say is that despite this polarized way of putting it, there are genuine values at stake on both sides.

The owls, on the one hand, are stand-ins for the values of the wild world, and specifically of the old-growth forests that are their only habitat. We respect their antiquity, their beauty, and indeed their sheer difference. We may even have the vague feeling that the possibility of our own lives being rich and rewarding is partly tied up with a richly varied natural world. On the other hand, we also care about preserving people's jobs and the communities that depend on the timber economy. We care about the quality of life that timber products make possible. Certainly sometimes we all need wood!

To deny or shrug off either set of concerns in the name of the other does not contribute to a better understanding or to a just solution. Can we instead go ahead together?

We could try to compromise. Again, this is not irresponsible or morally weak, especially not if done well. Since so little old-growth forest is left, for example, the health of the timber industry hardly depends upon it. Maybe no more needs to be cut at all. Other places could be cut instead. In fact, both sides could sometimes "win" if land were *traded*—if more ecologically or aesthetically vital land were preserved by trading less vital land for it. Precisely this policy was adopted by the Clinton Interior Department and (although criticized by some on both sides) has managed to somewhat defuse the "timber wars" in recent years.

Once again, though, we should be able to do better still. There may be more integrative possibilities. If we could create jobs based on owl-watching tourism, for instance, as has been done very successfully with whales, then owl interests and human interests might *converge* rather than diverge. Or again, we could seek to create a sustainable timber industry, using wood in a more intensive, craft-based way, rather than shipping massive amounts of raw wood abroad or pulping it for plywood, as the big timber corporations do at present. *That* kind of logging, unlike the present practice, would have a future: better for loggers *and* the forests.

Gun Control: A Dialogue

Thinking integratively takes some getting used to, and it's not always easy to stick to it, either, when you are dealing with people who picture moral debates only in polarized terms. Here's one example of how it might go in practice, with a new issue: gun control.

M: Are you for or against gun control?
P: Yes.

M: What do mean, "yes"? Yes or *no?* Which one? Whose side are you on?

P: I think that both sides are onto something. I favor some kinds of gun control, but I also think that gun control by itself partly misses the point.

M: In short, you don't really know what you think. Well, let me tell you . . .

P: I *do* know what I think. I think that both sides have some valid points. On the one hand, I think it's pretty clear that certain kinds of guns do much more harm than good: they make it too easy to kill, or are too prone to accidents. Nobody thinks young children should be dying in gun accidents. Banning or at least controlling certain kinds of guns would be a good start . . .

M: So you're for gun control! But if you ban some kinds of weapons then sooner or later we're going to ban all of them! Just let me tell you . . .

P: I don't see why we can't stop wherever we choose. The law already says that you can't own an atomic bomb or a bazooka or a flame-thrower. We already have gun control! We already ban some weapons without banning all.

M: Well, anyway, guns don't kill people, people kill people.

P: That's just a slogan, not very clear either. But I agree that in a deeper way, guns are usually not the real problem. If that's what the slogan really means. Usually the real problem is people's willingness to use such violence against each other in the first place.

M: So you're against gun control! Your head's on straight after all.

P: I am *for* some effective strategies for reducing violence and accidental shootings. Sometimes that means gun control; but it also means trying to address the underlying causes of killing.

M: I'm having a hard time getting a handle on what you think. It seems like you want to satisfy everybody.

P: Oh, terrible! Can't both sides be onto something?

M: You can't satisfy everybody. Get serious!

P: I'll try again. You want the freedom to own hunting rifles and collector's items. I doubt that people are getting murdered by those kinds of guns, so I don't see why you can't keep them. But the pro-control side wants to ban the handguns that are used in most murders, and lead to the most accidents, and I don't see why we can't do that too. Meanwhile, neither you nor I want to live in such a violent society, and I think if you really mean it about "people killing people," you'd be right there with me supporting the kinds of measures that might actually reduce violence. *You* get serious!

M: It's still wishy-washy. You need to take a stand.

P: I *am* taking a stand! I just don't think the only way to take a stand is to act like I have the whole truth to myself.

P and M obviously bring different assumptions about moral disagreements to this debate. P's attitude opens up the possibility of some genuine progress. Regions of disagreement will

---

Integrative Strategies at a Glance

- When truly opposite values conflict, we can at least *split the difference.*
- Different values may still be *compatible.* We can explore them with an eye to finding ways to satisfy both at the same time.
- Most disagreements are framed by deeper shared values. We can work from those shared values—from that *common ground*—toward jointly agreeable resolutions.

remain, of course—even fundamental disagreements. That's no reason not to try to do better everywhere else. There is plenty to do!

FOR PRACTICE AND THINKING ∿

Some Questions

Why do you think we polarize values? That is, why is it so tempting? Do you agree with the suggested explanations in this chapter? What else might be going on? What about *you*—how well can you resist the temptation? What are two or three practical ways in which you could help yourself and those around you to avoid polarizing values?

Practice

"Each side is right about *something*," I've insisted. Given our usual habits, it's a hard message to get. We're too used to debating polarized issues. Just the mere acknowledgment that the other side has some points needs a lot of practice.

So: identify your current position on some of the "hot-button" issues of the day. Now consider the opposite position—the other side or sides. Ask yourself *what the other side(s) is right about*—not wrong, but *right*. Where do you actually agree with them? What are their strongest and most important points?

It's tempting to answer by just summarizing what you think the other side thinks. "They think this; they think that." That's helpful too, but the task here is to go farther. What do they think *that you think too?* What do you actually think they're right about? Go beyond "I think . . . " and "They think . . . " to "We think . . . ." If you're in a group setting, a variation of this exercise is to make a list together of all of the relevant values that *both* (all) sides in some debate share, even if it seems at the beginning that none are shared at all. Usually you can come up with a very long list! That in itself should be surprising—and inspiring.

For a variation of this exercise, visit some parking lots and write down the bumperstickers on moral issues you see. Look for a wide range, including the ones that infuriate you. Now try to write alternative *integrative* bumperstickers. Is there a way to say something pithy that brings us together rather than divides us, that clarifies or connects rather than misrepresents and polarizes?

For example, you will discover a great deal of pro-choice and pro-life sloganizing. GOD HATES ABORTION, they say. ABORTION STOPS A BEATING HEART. On the other side, IF YOU'RE AGAINST ABORTION, DON'T HAVE ONE. So it was an inspiration one day to see EVERY CHILD A WANTED CHILD. Think of that: instead of trashing the other side for the evils of their ways, there is an appeal to the kind of value that unites us. It doesn't insist on one side over the other; it reminds us of what we should *all* aim for in the end. Every child a wanted child, which means: women have both the right and the responsibility to regulate pregnancy. Every child a wanted child, which means: when pregnancy occurs, we need to do everything we can to be sure the potential child *is* "wanted," that is, that the family can sustain the pregnancy and the child. The whole issue appears in a different light—and as a collective responsibility, an invitation to try to better the world.

Limits and Exceptions

Granting that there is something right about *most* sides of *most* debates, is this true of *all* sides in *all* debates? Is it always true that each side has a point?

I'm inclined to say yes, but then I've also been accused of being an overly generous person. What do *you* think?

Be careful not to say that there is nothing right about a certain moral position just because you disagree with its ultimate conclusion. Remember that people who draw different moral conclusions may still share many of the same moral values. They just balance them out differently. People who are pro-choice on abortion, for example, also value life—indeed may value it very highly—but still believe that in at least some situations choice must take precedence. The value of life remains a shared value, and one good starting point for working together.

Generosity also sometimes suggests looking "underneath" a moral position, even one we find repugnant, to ask what genuine needs or concerns may be motivating it. For example, hatred against other, "outside" groups may arise out of a deep sense of exclusion and disempowerment. And this too, before it settles on some scapegoat, could be a perfectly valid feeling. Just repressing the advocates of such evils leaves the attraction of the evil itself untouched. Repression may even drive it deeper, making it more attractive. Even here, then—even when we can genuinely speak of right versus *wrong*—we need to try to listen, to try to figure out the other side rather than just condemning it outright, and to try to figure out how the people involved can be reached.

So again: can you think of any considered moral position that is just flat-out completely *wrong,* with nothing redeeming whatsoever to be said for it? Take some time and care with this question. It's not at all as easy as it might look, however you answer.

NOTES

The quote from John Dewey is from his essay "The Construction of Good," Chapter 10 of his book *The Quest for Certainty,* reprinted in James Gouinlock, *The Moral Writings of John Dewey* (Macmillan, 1976), Chapter 5, where the quotation can be found on p. 154. The general theme of integrating values is thoroughly Deweyan, as Gouinlock's collection makes clear. See also my book *Toward Better Problems* (Temple University Press, 1992), as well as *A 21st Century Ethical Toolbox,* Chapter 7.

Roger Fisher and William Ury's book *Getting to Yes* (Penguin, 1983) is essential practical reading on integrating values. Also useful is Tom Rusk, *The Power of Ethical Persuasion* (Penguin, 1993).

On compromise, a careful philosophical treatment is Martin Benjamin's *Splitting the Difference* (University Press of Kansas, 1990). Benjamin systematically contests the various arguments that ethical philosophers have offered (or might offer—the arguments are seldom fully spelled out) against taking compromise seriously as a moral method. Given the plurality of values, Benjamin argues, what he calls "integrity-preserving compromise" is not only possible but sometimes even *required* in ethics.

Beware of the temptation, though, to reduce all integrative thinking to some form of compromise. Normally we can do much better than that. When compatible values are dovetailed, or when we work from common ground, we're not just "splitting the difference." Though the difference may remain, we may still be able to honor *all* of the values on both sides, to go much farther, as it were, than halfway. Compromise is nothing to be ashamed of, but it is still a kind of last resort; first there are more creative avenues to try.

There is also an intriguing social-psychological literature on integrative strategies, some of which suggests that competitive, polarized struggles can be defused simply by reconceptualizing the issues at hand as problems that are solvable in a cooperative and mutually acceptable way. The results are demonstrably better for everyone, even by crudely self-interested standards. See Dean Pruitt and Steven Lewis, "The Psychology of Integrative Bargaining," in Daniel Druckman, ed., *Negotiation: A Social-Psychological Perspective* (London: Sage Publications, 1977). For additional strategies see J. H. Carens, "Compromise in Politics," In J. R. Penlock and John Chapman, eds. *Compromise in Ethics, Law, and Politics* (New York University Press, 1979).

Time's "Owl versus Man" cover appeared on 25 June 1990. For background on the integrative approach to "Owls versus Man" suggested in the text, see the accompanying article (which, interestingly, is not at all as polarized as the cover suggests) and John B. Judis, "Ancient Forests, Lost Jobs," *In These Times* 14:31 (Aug. 1–14, 1990). Environmental ethics is discussed in more detail in *Toolbox*, Chapter 21. A thorough study concluding that environmentalism and economic welfare are *not* at odds—that in fact they go together— is Stephen Meyer, *Environmentalism and Economic Prosperity* (MIT Project on Environmental Politics and Policy, 1992).

On the values involved with the assisted suicide debate, see Margaret Battin, Rosamond Rhodes, and Anita Silvers, *Physician-Assisted Suicide: Expanding the Debate* (Routledge, 1998). For a Catholic approach that highlights assisted suicide as a communal challenge, see Richard Gula, *Euthanasia: Moral and Pastoral Perspectives* (Paulist Press, 1994). For the application of Kant's ethical theory to the question of suicide, see his *Grounding for the Metaphysics of Morals,* James Ellington, trans (Hackett, 1981), p. 36. Kant does not mean that we must live passively in the face of suffering—just that ending our lives to escape the suffering is not one of our moral options.

Secular ethical theories and traditional moral systems lie mostly outside the scope of this book, but I suspect that many readers have studied or are currently studying them with other texts. In this book I am concerned mainly with giving them a place among our other practical tools without making them too central either. Certainly they have their uses as ways of articulating values; and they can make connections and open up vistas we otherwise would never reach. On the other hand, people sometimes appeal to theories to justify their favorite values and then try to rule the competing values out of court entirely. In this case, polarized values on the practical level are only restated, in a more formal, abstract, and thus more entrenched and resistant way, on the theoretical level. For a sobering discussion of this process at work in medical ethics, see Richard Zaner, *Ethics and the Clinical Encounter* (Prentice-Hall, 1988), Chapter 1.

Chapters 5 and 6 of *Toolbox* discuss the role and possibilities of ethical theories in much more detail, though even there I can only scratch the surface. Some theories claim to assimilate all other values and moral principles under a single, all-inclusive criterion of value: these are usually the "utilitarian" theories that aim to maximize satisfaction or happiness as the ultimate good. Other theories claim priority for rights or duties, or perhaps the virtues. All of this is controversial, but it is safe to say that none of these theoretical claims has been firmly established. Ethical theories, though useful, still need to be approached with caution. Note that I am not at all arguing that theory itself must be rejected: the point is rather that it's wisest to let theories counterbalance and limit each other's claims. Multiplying perspectives on a single issue need not hinder problem-solving at all—quite the contrary, as this chapter has tried to argue.

To explore an integrative approach to the abortion issue, see *Toolbox*, Chapter 17 and the reading by Roger Rosenblatt in Chapter 7. The reading for *Toolbox* Chapter 14 comes from a remarkable organization called The Common Ground Network for Life and Choice, formed in 1994 to bring together activists from the opposing sides in the abortion conflict in the hopes of creating real dialogue, understanding each other better, and finding common ground that the two sides could build upon together rather than frustrating each other's every move. They're still going strong—and the common ground approach is now being generalized to other issues. For more information, check out the Network's website at <www.searchforcommonground.org>.

5

ETHICS WITH A HEART

~

Ethics asks us to resist closed-heartedness; to keep the heart open. This too is a kind of mindfulness—perhaps it is the most fundamental kind of all—and it is the last of our major themes in practical ethics.

WHEN THE HEART CLOSES

You are being served at a restaurant—or bank, ticket window, checkout counter, or any of a dozen other such places. Everyone knows how automatic and taken-for-granted such a relationship can be. Indeed, it is seldom a "relationship" at all. For customers, all too often, waiters are just a way of getting food. For waiters, a customer may be just another mouth and a tip. This can be true even if there is some dialogue or maybe even flirtation going on. Each may just be playing a role, with hardly a thought for the *person* on the other side.

What is happening here? In cases like these, we seem to be unable to project ourselves into others' situations, unwilling to imagine others' feelings as if they were ours. The nineteenth-century philosopher Josiah Royce describes it almost biblically:

> Thou hast regarded [thy neighbor's] thought, his feeling, as somehow different from thine. Thou hast said, "A pain in him is not like a pain in me, but something far easier to bear." He seems to thee a little less living than thou . . . . So, dimly and by instinct hast thou lived with thy neighbor, and hast known him not, being blind. Thou hast made [of him] a thing, no Self at all.

This is what it means to have a closed heart. To put it in a more modern way, closed-heartedness is our tendency to forget that the people around us have the same kinds of expectations and needs as we do ourselves. It is our tendency to treat others like things, like servants or obstacles, rather than truly like other people.

Oh, someone will say, that's too extreme. We certainly do know, all the time or most of the time, that other people are people too.

But consider: we hardly even notice when human bank tellers are replaced with automatic teller machines. Why? Just possibly because we were treating the tellers like machines all along? This is what Royce means when he says that we live with each other "dimly and by instinct." We treat others like things, as if they had "no Self at all." Too often we relate to each other out of pure habit, automatically.

Royce is even literally right when he says that we discount other people's pain. Think of what happens when doctors suddenly become patients: when surgeons go under the knife or anesthesiologists get anesthesia. A common reaction is shock.

The injection that for years they told patients "just hurts a little" turns out to hurt like hell. Procedures that are routine to them suddenly become frightening and new. The attitudes of other doctors—their own attitudes too, until that very moment—begin to seem strange and hardhearted.

Why didn't they see it before? After all, they're only experiencing the same thing they've seen for years, just from a different point of view. But sometimes it seems that point of view is everything. As the old joke goes, when (some) doctors say "it won't hurt at all," what they really mean is that it won't hurt *them*. (Royce again: "Thou hast said, 'A pain in him is not like a pain in me, but something far easier to bear'"). For too many doctors, patients' pain is something to be "managed," not something to be shared and sympathized with.

We recognize and resent this kind of closed-heartedness when we're on the receiving end. Nothing is so chilling as knowing that you are only a "thing" for someone else. Cheery salespeople greet me on the phone like their long-lost brother but hang up in mid-sentence when they realize that they are not going to make a sale. And it gets much worse. Sexual exploitation—realizing that you are only a "body" for someone else, only a means to someone else's momentary pleasure—is far more deeply chilling. All trust, all sense of standing as one person among others, is betrayed. We complain, as Royce did, that "you're just treating me like an object," or "like a thing, not a person."

Cases in which people are completely reduced to "things" are among the greatest of evils. The Nazi concentration camps were meant to dehumanize: they were deliberately designed as the first step to mass slaughter. Slavery meant the literal treatment of human beings as no more than property, and was partly rationalized by the claim that blacks did not really feel physical pain or suffer under oppression in the ways whites would (once again:"A pain in him is not like a pain in me ..."). It has been said many times, of many people and peoples. Several centuries of scientists said it, and some still say it, of other animals. Closed-heartedness is tempting—and all too common.

Why the Heart Closes

To resist the closing of our hearts we must understand why it happens. Here are some of the ways.

The primary villain, according to many moral philosophers, is self-centeredness. We don't see or hear others because our own selves loom so large. Sometimes we simply ignore others, are oblivious to them, so full are we with our selves. This is why some people can live for years in a family or other group and yet never have a clue about what anyone else is feeling. What they themselves are feeling is just too important.

Self-centeredness also leads us to read into others what we want to see there. A man wants the object of his desire to feel the same toward him; therefore he concludes that she does. He is not interested in, and in fact may be a little afraid of, finding out what she really thinks.

So self-centeredness is part of the story. But there are other factors too, factors that may be equally important. For one, there is simple practical need. Life is too complicated and too demanding for us always to relate in a completely connected way. We do need to get our food at the restaurant and our money at the bank, and maybe even to sell each other things over the phone. Sometimes we probably do have to live with each other "dimly and by instinct," as Royce puts it, relating to other people, even our closest family and friends, a little automatically, a little "blindly." Sometimes. The problem comes when we relate to other people *only* in this automatic way.

Habit takes over. When we relate to more and more people as if they were automatic teller machines or patients to be "managed," we may lose the ability to relate in any other way.

Disparaging language and stereotypes also play a variety of roles in closing our hearts. Sometimes our language literally reduces a person, or a whole group of people, to things. When men refer to women by their sexual parts, for example, they treat women as "sex objects"—that is, as objects, bodies, to be used for sexual purposes. Common slang words for women, like "chick," "babe," or "doll," name mindless or helpless playthings or dependents. These terms teach all of us, men and women alike, to *see* women in that way.

Stereotypes call forth routine and immediate responses, again keeping us from relating to other people as people, and substituting automatic responses. Imagine encountering someone completely new, about whom we have no preconceptions or expectations. Here is someone to whom we actually need to *relate*. This is very different from what usually happens. Usually we come well equipped with labels. All we need to know is that someone is a Republican or homeless or a lawyer or even just a stranger, and we think we know "who they are." Appearance alone is often enough to bring out the stereotypes. No need to relate; just react.

Self-fulfilling Prophecies

Stereotypes also can become self-fulfilling. For example, one of the chief excuses for the enslavement of blacks in America was that black people were naturally "ignorant and depraved." But one of the prime effects of slavery was that the slaves were often *made* ignorant and depraved. They were kept unschooled and stultified with work, their families and communities broken again and again. Thus, as antislavery campaigner

Frederick Douglass pointed out, "the very crimes of slavery become slavery's best defense. By making the enslaved a character fit only for slavery, they excuse themselves for failing to make the slave a freeman." Slavery wears down and degrades the slave; then this very degradation is blamed on the slaves themselves (it's said to be "their nature"), thus justifying more slavery and still more degradation.

Much the same can be said, in a milder way perhaps, about the effects of other kinds of prejudice. Sexism, for example, can also become a self-fulfilling prophecy. All manner of prejudicial barriers wear down and consume a woman, and then her own failures are held up as proof that sexism is justified.

There are also examples beyond the sphere of human relations. Think of animals in "factory farms": treated like living egg or milk machines, or living pieces of meat, unable in many cases even to turn around or follow any of their instincts. Soon they genuinely *become* unsociable, incapable, and pitiful—not to mention dangerous to themselves and others. People who know such animals are often genuinely puzzled about how anyone could think that they have "rights" or moral standing— the animals seem so pitiful. But the fact that the animals are reduced to such a state is precisely the objection. They are *made* pitiful. And then their degradation naturally seems to justify still more degrading treatment.

HOW THE HEART OPENS

Royce goes on:

> Have done with this illusion, and simply try to learn the truth. Pain is pain, joy is joy, everywhere, even as in thee . . . . In all exultation and hope, everywhere, from the noblest to the lowest, the same conscious, burning, willful life is found, endlessly manifold as the forms of the living creatures, unquenchable as

the fires of the sun, real as these impulses that even now throb in thine own heart.

Remaining open to this fact I will call *open-heartedness*. To put it in a more modern way, open-heartedness is our ability to remember that the people around us have the same kinds of expectations and needs as we do ourselves. It is to know, and not just say, that other people *are* people too.

Recognizing when and why we often close our hearts is a start toward opening them back up. We can acknowledge our own self-centeredness but then put it in its place. We can take more care with our language. We can take our stereotypes with more than a few grains of salt. We can try to break some of our habitual and automatic ways of relating to other people. Treat the waitress like a person (how would you feel if you were in her shoes?) rather than a food-toting robot or someone whose purpose in life is to meet your needs.

With the question, "How would you feel if you were in her shoes?" we come back to the old Golden Rule. I said in Chapter 2 that the Golden Rule is not really a "rule" at all in the sense that it gives us a way to make specific decisions. But it has other uses. To say, "Do unto others as you would have them do unto you," is essentially to say: remember that, in the big picture, others are just as real, just as conscious, just as important as you are. And that is a crucial reminder. It is one important way past our self-centeredness.

My ethics classes help staff several shelters for homeless people in the cities near our college. We go into the shelters with anxieties, self-conscious, carrying the culture's baggage of images and media stereotypes. We come out seeing something different. One student wrote after her first visit:

All of my insecurities were running through my head as I approached the door and had to be let in by one of the guests.

Some people were gathered by the TV and it's funny to me now, but the first thing I thought was, "Hey, I watch that show too!" It's embarrassing to look back now at how nervous I was because then it hit me that homeless people are just the same as me . . . . Right away I was so glad I had come.

"Just the same as me"—that's the starting point. Not that there are no differences, but rather that our differences can be honored on the basis of our underlying commonality, rather than commonality denied on the basis of difference. As the Shelter's eloquent volunteer statement concludes: "Our guests, in short, are just like us, only they are more poor, under stress, and are forced to make more difficult choices than most of us face."

Notice that term "guests," too. "All people who come are guests," the statement says. Not "homeless," not even "clients"— that's social-service agency talk. No: guests, fellow human beings, whom it is a privilege to help.

Be prepared for surprises. One way to a closed heart, remember, is sheer habit: our tendency to relate to others automatically and out of stereotype and routine. To open our hearts we need to take the opposite tack. Break the routine. Deliberately look for what goes against the stereotypes. Remind yourself that you do *not* know everything there is to know about a person just on the basis of his or her appearance or a few labels. I have learned more from my mentally retarded brother than from many of my teachers. But to most people he is just "retarded." They can't see past the label. Likewise, no one is just a "chick" or a lawyer or a fundamentalist—any more than *you* could be reduced to such a label. Be prepared to notice!

Learn to keep still sometimes. One of the chief obstacles to really seeing or hearing other people is all the interference coming from ourselves. Train yourself to turn it off for a while. You can always turn it back on later (if you want to). But when you are listening, listen wholeheartedly. Don't judge—just listen.

Reach out to others. Give people a chance. Remember the ways in which patterns of closed-heartedness can become self-fulfilling. Then consider the parallel point, that patterns of *open*-heartedness can become self-fulfilling too. So say hello to people on the street, and see what kind of good will comes back to you. Offer a troubled child or a troubled friend some love or trust, rather than just moralizing in the hopes that maybe someday they will deserve it. *You* take the first step. Trust first—invite them to live up to it.

In a burst of inspiration, someone once set up a program at an urban senior center that brings in ex-convicts, their last shot at rehabilitation, to help the elderly. "Because maybe this center's a last shot for some of these old folks too. Last shot for companionship, last shot before dying, alone. Both groups on the edge—why not bring them together?" So an ex-con and an old woman walk down the street together. She was once mugged by someone like him. Now he helps with the shopping. She says:

> I don't know what he sees in me. All I know, he walks me home. We talk and joke. I learn things about how things are in the world now, which I don't know much about anymore. And I don't get the feeling that I'm just a little old Jewish lady. You think that's nothing? You know how many other people I don't feel like a little old lady with?

He says:

> Try to shake having been a junkie and done time, man. Everywhere you go, you get that. But this woman, it's like she doesn't care. She says she had a hard life too, maybe that's it. I told her how I robbed things. I told her about jail. She says, "Your mother must have been very upset. Let's get groceries. You

have time to do that?" Nobody ever treated me like I had anything to give. Just to take. So that's all I ever did. Take . . .

"It's a chance to break out of the old patterns," says the founder of the program. No kidding. Chances were taken all around. Give people a chance; take a chance yourself . . .

THE EXPANDING CIRCLE

It is because ethics calls for open-heartedness that ethics is also open-*ended.* The circle of our ethical concern tends to grow: to become more and more inclusive.

There was a time when moral concern only went as far as the walls of a man's city. Indeed, it didn't even go that far, as women, children, slaves, and non–property-owning males within the walls didn't count either. Gradually some of these others came to be recognized as moral equals, but each step was a fight. The abolition of slavery took centuries. Deeply rooted forms of racism and sexism still persist. So does suspicion of outsiders—those not of "our" race or nation or culture—and the willingness to abandon them to whatever misery fate may impose on them.

Moral growth in such cases is much more of a struggle than it may seem after the fact. Take slavery for example. From slave-owners' point of view, it was simply unthinkable that slaves could somehow be their moral equals, deserving the same kind of human respect. Slavery was taken for granted. It was embraced and practiced by all the right people. The science and religion of the day both rationalized it. As Frederick Douglass pointed out, slavery so degraded the enslaved people that their enslavement could really seem to be justified. They did not seem like equals. That slavery could be called into question was unimaginable—until it was.

How did the question even arise? As in any major social change, there were a variety of reasons. For one thing, not everyone in slave societies had a stake in slavery. In the United States in the mid-nineteenth century, major economic interests had begun to push the other way. Also, at least a few parts of the dominant moral and religious traditions had always spoken out against slavery. There were periodic slave revolts too, though they were violently put down.

Beneath and beyond these forces, though, a basic moral process was also at work. Some people—at first only a few—were willing and able to identify with the enslaved race: to put themselves into the position of a slave, to see enslaved people as people like themselves, suffering as they themselves would. They began to question the "obvious" idea that race could make such an enormous moral difference that people of one race could be free and another enslaved. Gradually they found a voice and went to work on the hearts and minds of others. The old excuses began to ring hollow.

Great forces are in tension at moments like this. On the one side, the old habits and norms remain powerful. No one wants to think that whole ways of life, ways of life that are comfortable and "normal" to most people, may still prove morally unacceptable and have to change. Yet our hearts may pull us in another direction. It may become more and more apparent that the old ways have to change.

Philosopher Tom Regan wonders what he would have done in the days when the religious and scientific rationalizations for slavery were still widely accepted:

I play this question over and over again in my imagination. I know what I want to believe. I want to believe that I would have been one among those who agitated for change in the moral status quo—one among the minority who saw through the flimsy fabric of prejudice, ignorance, and fear that barred acceptance of all humans as morally equal, each to all. But ... I do not know. The power of the dominant culture ... is great ....

There is no reliable guide in such situations. But we can at least recognize that sometimes the "moral status quo" may be wrong—and recognize that sometimes the heart tells us first. Be ready to listen.

Is the moral status quo anywhere in question today? Regan thinks so. Consider, he says, our treatment of other animals. We are used to thinking of animals as lesser creatures, indeed hardly as creatures at all: as mere resources available to serve our needs. Commercially raised chickens spend the whole of their short lives in cages too small to allow them even to turn around. Veal calves are deprived of nutrients, exercise, even light. Large numbers of dogs, chimps, cats, rabbits, and many other animals are used each year to test new drugs and chemicals for eventual human use.

Yet the plight of these animals has begun to speak to us. Here too, some people have been willing and able to listen: to put themselves into the position of other beings, to see other animals as beings like ourselves, suffering as we would. They are beginning to question the "obvious" idea that species could make such an enormous moral difference that beings of one species could be morally special while those of all other species could be mercilessly exploited. Perhaps they are wrong—perhaps other animals really do not deserve full-fledged moral consideration—but their voices are certainly becoming harder to rationalize away.

All the old dismissals of animals are still with us. Animals can't think, people say; they don't feel pain, and on and on. For most people eating animals is still so normal as to seem unquestionable. Many of my students literally believe that they cannot live without it. But people are changing too. Vegetarianism is on the rise, and most restaurants now serve non-meat dishes. The old habits may no longer be good enough. Even people who continue to eat meat are beginning to feel obliged to make excuses for it, which is at least a sign that they feel some tension. Moral unease is growing. Perhaps in a hundred years we will find the current treatment of animals utterly unbelievable, much as we now find slavery unbelievable. Or perhaps we won't. In any case, the question is now open.

Ethics is also trying to respond to the environmental crisis. Some philosophers and moralists are arguing that we must begin to view *all* of nature ethically. Perhaps we must now take a new look not merely at other animals but at whole ecosystems, even at the whole living Earth. The circle may grow very wide indeed.

Here crisis pushes us, to be sure, but once again there is a "pull" too. We are beginning to recognize the enormous creativity, complexity, and depth of the rest of the world: the nonhuman, the other-than-human, the more-than-human. The grandeur and magic of nature, the silence-that-is-not-stillness of the wild, the glittering stars, feather-borne singers everywhere, the very continents gliding about on molten oceans of rock; and on and on. It has been easy to overlook all of this, to ignore it, to turn a blind eye to it even when it is right next to us: and therefore we also easily destroy it. Human exploitation of nature has been with us a long time. It too is a habit, a comfortable, normal way of life. Yet it too is now being questioned. Twenty years ago we could not have imagined even something now as basic as recycling bins in everyone's basement or whale songs on CD. Who knows what another twenty years will bring? A new period of unimagined moral growth may be upon us.

So ethics is not a closed book. Our values, and our ways of living them out, have changed many times, and will change again. The circle is expanding, and our sympathies and our understanding behind its leading edge are expanding and deepening too. This is part of what makes ethics so difficult—and so exciting. Stay with it. And keep both an open heart and an open mind.

For Practice and Thinking ～

Some Questions

This chapter highlights some forms of closed-heartedness and suggests some explanations for them. Do any of these apply to you? Which ones? To your friends? Which ones? How do you think these forms of closed-heartedness arise?

Now consider the same questions for *open*-heartedness.

Get Out There and Do Something

There is no substitute for actually going out and helping. Find a way to help that is genuinely face to face. Tutor a struggling child. Volunteer at a local homeless shelter or soup kitchen. Work with retarded citizens. Read to children at an inner-city child care. Teach a class at a community center or a nursing home. Help build a house with Habitat for Humanity.

Making the arrangements may take only a phone call. Most homeless shelters are desperate for volunteer help and have staff coordinators to arrange volunteers' dates and times. When floods or storms strike, many cities or counties set up volunteer hotlines to match willing volunteers with people in need of help. Community newspapers often run appeals for help. School offices schedule community volunteers and tutors. Most colleges and universities have offices that match community organizations' needs and student volunteers. Find yours and use it.

As the Circle Expands

When we begin to speak of values at or beyond the "edge" of the expanding moral circle, we often find that we do not yet have the language we need. Sometimes it takes a while for moral language to catch up to the imagination.

On the other hand, we do not always have the luxury of waiting. Parts of the more-than-human world—other animals and natural environments—are in serious danger. We may need to be able to give them a moral voice right now.

So: practice writing a letter to your senator about some natural area you know and love. How do you convey its value in a few paragraphs? Practice telling a friend the same thing. Don't overlook less familiar means of expression, like nature writing or poetry. Are there other kinds of lyrical or religious expression you'd want to use too? (How do you *feel* in the presence of animal eyes, or summer thunderstorms in the woods, or the ocean at dawn . . . ?) And are there other (possibly still more creative and unexpected) means of expression yet? Environmental activists sometimes use costume, ritual, and dance, as well as chaining themselves to polluting pipes or living in trees to keep them from being cut down or interposing themselves in little boats between whales and whale hunters. Aren't they trying to convey nature's values in symbolic ways? Sometimes people even attempt to speak for other life forms by speaking *as* those life forms (or for that matter as rocks, rivers, and so on). What else might *you* suggest?

NOTES

The quotes from Josiah Royce are from *The Religious Aspect of Philosophy* (Boston: Houghton Mifflin Company, 1885), pp. 157–162. For further reading along these lines, more difficult but also more suggestive, try Martin Buber, *I and Thou*, Walter Kaufmann, trans. (W.W. Norton and Company).

On sexual language as stereotyping, see Robert Baker, "'Chicks' and 'Pricks': A Plea for Persons," in Robert Baker and Frederick Elliston, eds., *Philosophy and Sex* (Prometheus Books, 1975). The citation from Frederick Douglass on p. 74 is from his speech, "The Claims of the Negro Ethnologically Considered," in *The Frederick Douglass Papers,* ser. 1, vol. 2 (Yale University Press, 1982), p. 507.

For more on self-fulfilling prophecies in ethics, see my paper, "Self-Validating Reduction: Toward a Theory of the Devaluation of Nature," *Environmental Ethics* 18 (1996):115–132, and pp. 94–105 of my book *Back to Earth: Tomorrow's Environmentalism* (Temple University Press, 1994).

On service as a form of ethical learning, see my *A 21st Century Ethical Toolbox,* Chapter 15, and Ram Dass and Paul Gorman, *How Can I Help? Stories And Reflections on Service* (Knopf, 1994). The account of the ex-cons at the senior center is one of many stories in Dass and Gorman's wonderful book: pp. 231–235.

The image of an expanding ethical circle was used by Peter Singer in a book by the same title: *The Expanding Circle* (Farrar, Straus, and Giroux, 1981), pp. 111–124. Singer's book *Animal Liberation* (rev. ed., Avon, 1991), along with Tom Regan's *The Case for Animal Rights* (University of California Press, 1983), are the classic philosophical defenses of the ethical status of other animals. For a richly textured and less theoretical approach to other animals, see Mary Midgley's work, for example *Animals and Why They Matter* (University of Georgia Press, 1983). The citation from Regan on p. 79–80 is from an unpublished paper called "Patterns of Resistance: The Struggle for Freedom and Equality in America," quoted by permission.

On the extension of ethics to the whole of the ecosphere, the classic source is Aldo Leopold, *Sand County Almanac* (New York: Oxford University Press, 1949). The opening of the last essay in that book, "The Land Ethic," also calls upon the image of an expanding circle. See also *Toolbox,* Chapter 21. My book *Back to Earth,* cited above, represents an experience-based approach to "expanding circles." See also my collection *An Invitation to Environmental Philosophy* (Oxford University Press, 1999); don't overlook its extensive bibliographic essay.

APPENDIX

How to Write an Ethics Paper

This book presents ethics primarily as a mode of action, and accordingly we have been concerned mainly with practical skills. In academic contexts, however, ethics is usually taught as a subject matter, and one of the primary skills called into play is writing. This appendix therefore offers some guidelines for writing an ethics paper.

GETTING STARTED

The first rule in writing any academic paper is: *understand the assignment*. You need to understand what kind of audience you should address, and what topic or range of topics should be covered.

You will almost always write more clearly and consistently if you keep in mind a vivid picture of a person or kind of person for whom you are writing. Besides, it is much easier to imagine yourself talking to your roommate, and maybe even your senator, than writing into an abstract void. So pick someone to write to. It may even be an actual person who will read your paper.

In one sense, obviously, you are writing for your teacher or professor. That is the bottom line. But he or she is usually not the best audience to keep in mind as you write. What you may need to say in your paper is not necessarily what you would say to your teacher in direct conversation. For example, teachers generally expect that student papers will competently review the subject matter, but the subject will seldom be news to the teacher. You need to imagine writing to someone who could use the explanation. I ask my students to imagine writing for a friend or roommate who is not in the class but who is, like them, intelligent and interested.

A specific topic may be assigned by your teacher, or the choice of topic may be left to you. If the choice is left to you, pick something that actually interests you, and about which you can say something constructive. After all, ethics is about real life: pick a real topic. If you are not sure whether a given topic is appropriate, ask.

Once you know your audience and topic, your next step is to choose a voice. By this I mean that you must decide *how* to write the paper. Are you going to summarize the state of an argument in a professional voice? Are you going to tell a story that makes a point? Will there be a place for humor? For the personal? To express uncertainty?

Many professors expect a kind of abstract and impersonal writing as a matter of course. Many philosophers tend to expect an argumentative style as well. Many, however, do not. Don't assume that these are your only options. For example, don't assume that you must write in the same style as the articles and arguments you may have been reading in class. Sometimes the point of a writing assignment is to *react* to such readings. It may be most effective and appropriate to react in a rather different style.

Often you discover what and how you are going to write only by actually writing. You do not need to decide for sure before you even start. Just start. Imagine yourself speaking to the person or audience for whom you have decided to write, and see what happens. Of course, the virtue of doing this in your imagination (and, when writing, in very rough form) is that you can start over—perhaps many times. Expect to write more than one draft (this book, for example, has gone through about twenty-five). You might try out several voices as you begin to write a few paragraphs, and see which approach has the best "feel." For more on writing and "voice," see Part VI of Peter Elbow's *Writing with Power* (Oxford University Press, 1981). On the matter of audience in particular, see Elbow's Chapter 20.

ARGUMENT PAPERS

In the remainder of this appendix, I outline two quite different possible styles for ethics papers, and offer specific guidelines for each. I begin with the *argument paper.*

An argument paper in ethics is an attempt to define an ethical position carefully and to defend or criticize it using the most general and plausible arguments you can find. It is a paper whose aim is to prove a point.

Here are a few general guidelines for argument papers.

1. Whether you are advancing your own argument or criticizing someone else's, do so in an orderly way. Don't jump right into criticism, or start by assuming the moral position that you want to try to establish. Start out with a little back-

ground on the issue (remember your audience). Summarize the argument you want to advance before developing it. Summarize it again when you are done.

If you are criticizing an argument, it is especially important to outline the argument before you begin to criticize it. Be sure to get it right. It is pointless to attack a position so extreme that no one holds it. Take some time to explain the argument, explore in what ways it is plausible (there must be something plausible about it if people find it persuasive), and cite and perhaps quote some of its advocates. *Then* you are ready for criticism. Once again, it is helpful to summarize your criticism before you begin and again when you are done.

2. Moral arguments are partly factual arguments, so another necessary rule is: get your facts straight. Arguments about our treatment of other animals, for example, should include some relevant facts and statistics about how animals are treated. Arguments about assisted suicide should give a short history of this procedure and an up-to-date legal report. You will need to do some research.

Take care at this stage. Remember that, in ethics in particular, strong opinions may color the facts. Certainly they color presentations of the facts. So use a variety of sources, use reliable sources, carefully check the citations for any factual claims that are central to your argument or seem debatable (and cite the best sources in your own paper), and watch the reasoning, especially if the argument makes statistical claims or claims about causes. Arguments of this sort can be complex, uncertain, and tricky. An argument guide is useful here: see, for example, my *Rulebook for Arguments* (Hackett Publishing Company), and (still briefer) *A 21st Century Ethical Toolbox,* Chapter 8.

3. A somewhat less obvious but crucial rule is: clarify the principles upon which your argument is based.

Your ethics course will probably introduce and examine some common ethical principles and illustrate the process of clarifying and reasoning about them. They may range from the fairly specific (like "Be honest on your taxes") to something quite general (like "Cause no unnecessary suffering") to the first principles of ethical theories (like "Seek the happiness of the greatest number").

Careful formulation of such principles is difficult. For example, fundamental legal issues often arise because it is unclear how existing legal principles apply to new situations. We have, for instance, a principle of parental rights. Legally, parents can decide where their underage children will live, what religion they grow up in or whether they grow up in any religion at all, whether they go to public schools or elsewhere (though not *whether* their children get educated), and so on. Still, there are areas of uncertainty. Can parents decide to deny their underage children life-saving medical treatment? What about Jehovah's Witnesses, who legally can refuse blood transfusions for themselves on religious grounds? Can they also refuse blood transfusions for their underage children?

In cases like this, it is not enough to offer some vague generalization about "parental rights" as the relevant ethical or legal principle. The entire matter turns on exactly—and I mean *exactly*—what such principles say. Precisely how far do parental rights extend?

Your job addressing such a case is to try to formulate a precise enough general principle to answer the specific question posed (such as, "Should people with religious objections to blood transfusions be allowed to refuse transfusions not only for themselves but also for their underage children?"). Your principle must *plausibly* answer the question. And it must not *im*plausibly answer other practical questions that might be addressed to it.

For example, if you conclude that parents ought to be allowed to refuse such treatments because "Parents have the right to make *all* fundamental religious choices for their underage children," then you may have indeed formulated a precise enough principle to answer the question. (You will need, though, to explain what you mean by "fundamental religious choice.") The principle may be plausible (argue for it). You might argue that the conclusion is plausible too. How, you might ask, could the law justifiably force blood into their bodies against the religious beliefs that are followed by their parents and that the children themselves very likely will accept as their own?

But this principle might have implausible implications as well. What if some parents' religion includes ritual torture, or severe fasting? These are called "counter-examples": possible cases where your proposed principle leads to implausible, or allegedly implausible, consequences.

Your task in the face of such counter-examples is either to amend your proposed principle (and then consider whether its implications change in the original case, for example with respect to refusing transfusions) or to defend its apparently implausible implications: to argue that the alleged counter-example doesn't refute the principle. (See my *Rulebook for Arguments,* section 11.) If you are criticizing someone else's argument, by contrast, arguing by counter-example may be exactly the strategy you want.

Again, this is a difficult matter, more difficult than any short discussion such as this one can explain. If your teacher expects you to argue in this style in your paper, your assigned readings and class work should offer you some practice and models to follow. For another model, or if no model is readily available, look at Peter Singer's chapter "Rich and Poor" in his book *Practical Ethics* (Cambridge University Press, 1979), widely reprinted in ethics textbooks and anthologies under similar titles. Singer's paper is a classic of the argument style. He uses several widely agreeable moral principles and analogies to argue that we have an obligation to give some of our time and resources to help people who are starving (that is, helping them is not just nice, but is *required*). You may or may not agree with him; I mention his article here because his style is widely admired and emulated.

A response to Singer is John Arthur, "World Hunger and Moral Obligation," in Christina Hoff Sommers, ed., *Vice and Virtue in Everday Life* (Harcourt Brace, 1996), an anthology that also includes Singer's piece. For other good examples of the argument style in ethics, see Colin McGinn's lively and rigorously argued little book, *Moral Literacy* (Hackett/Duckworth, 1992). Another classic article, more difficult, is Judith Thompson's "A Defense of Abortion," also included in Sommers and in a wide variety of other collections. Thompson relies on several striking analogies to defend a woman's right to choose abortion even if the fetus also has a right to life—not an easy point to argue!

DISCOVERY PAPERS

A *discovery paper* in ethics is an expression or exploration of an ethical position, usually linked to important events in the narrator's life or in our common experience. Often a discovery paper is a personal narrative or story, offered partly as a self-explanation and partly as an invitation for others to recognize something similar in their own experience.

We might take as an example a famous short essay by the novelist Alice Walker, "Am I Blue?," which can be found in her collection *Living by the Word* (Harcourt Brace Jovanovich,

1988). It's very brief, only five pages or so, which describe her encounters with a horse named Blue and some of the thoughts and changes that resulted. Blue came to live in a field near her home. She fed him apples from a tree next to the field, where, she says, "I remained as thrilled as a child by his flexible dark lips, huge, cubelike teeth that crunched the apples, core and all, with such finality, and his high, broad-breasted enormity; beside which, I felt small indeed." But

> Blue was lonely. Blue was horribly lonely and bored . . . . Five acres to tramp by yourself, endlessly, even in the most beautiful of meadows . . . cannot provide many interesting events, and once rainy season turned to dry that was about it . . . . I had forgotten that human animals and nonhuman animals can communicate quite well; if we are brought up around animals as children we take this for granted. It is in [animals'] nature to express themselves. What else are they going to express? And, generally speaking, they are ignored. (p. 5)

She begins to muse on the parallels to the treatment of black slaves, Indians, and sometimes the young: ignored too. The very possibility that they might have something of their own to communicate is often denied. Too often we see only our own reflections in those we subordinate and oppress.

She travels for a time. When she returns, Blue has a companion. "There was a new look in his eyes. A look of independence, of self-possession, of inalienable *horse*ness." There are weeks of a deep and mutual feeling of justice and peace. But eventually Blue's companion becomes pregnant. It turns out that she was "put with him" for that purpose. She is taken away.

> Blue was like a crazed person. Blue *was,* to me, a crazed person. He galloped furiously . . . around and around his five acres. He whinnied until he couldn't. He tore the ground with his

hooves . . . . He looked always and always toward the road down which his partner had gone. And then, occasionally . . . , he looked at me. It was a look so piercing, so full of grief, a look so *human,* that I almost laughed (I felt too sad to cry) to think there are people who do not know animals suffer. (p. 7)

But they do. Again she is led to think about the suffering all around us, and how too often we evade or deny that communication. The conclusion then is quick and stunning:

As we talked of freedom and justice one day for all, we sat down to steaks. I am eating misery, I thought, as I took the first bite. And spit it out. (p. 8)

Something happened here. Thinking about Blue helped Walker to draw connections between the experiences of human oppression that, as a black woman activist, she knew so well, and our exploitation of other animals. It was not merely abstract, either: Walker came to see her own actions in a different light, and the result was that at that moment she stopped eating meat.

Of course, as I said about views like Singer's and Thompson's, you may not agree with the bottom line. In the same situation, you might have done something different. The point is that ethical discoveries do happen. You do not have to write as well as Walker either, of course, but you should try to capture the freshness and directness of your own experiences in the same way. A discovery paper is an exploration of when such things have happened for *you.*

Here are a few guidelines for discovery papers.

1. Don't sentimentalize. You are writing about experience and what it meant to you, so you must speak the language of feeling, but that does not mean that everything must be described in terms of feeling or that the paper can simply "emote." Notice that Walker is carefully descriptive even when

she is speaking of highly emotional matters, for example of Blue after his companion was taken away. Also, she is always drawing connections. The theme of animal communication, for example, runs through her essay, and it is this that makes the last lines so natural. So don't just tell us what you felt; tell us what happened, and what thoughts it provoked, so that we may begin to think and feel and maybe even act the same way.

2. Draw conclusions. Though the discovery style is much more personal than the argumentative style, remember that you are writing about the experience of values for a reason. You are not just reporting on yourself, but opening up the question of moral change and growth by so doing. You are suggesting, at least indirectly, that here are some questions that need moral attention, or here are some possibilities—new attitudes, new ways of life—that may call to us ethically.

For example, Walker is posing a very specific question: how it is that we can so completely close our hearts to other creatures, and what we might do if our hearts were a little more open. Notice how beautifully her title opens that question. Am I Blue?, she asks. That is: in what ways is she herself, like Blue, a covictim of oppression? The other side of the question is: how is she also like the oppressors? And what should she do about that? Part of her answer is to put down her fork.

In general, then, explore what you think are the larger implications of your experience. How did it change your sense of values? Why did it do this? How do these conclusions relate to the sense of values you took into the experience? How do they relate to traditional values? And what did you, or should you, do about it? Your conclusions need not be extensive, but some attention to these questions is necessary.

Discovery papers are not argument papers (though you could combine the two styles, starting for example with a discovery and ending by trying to make moral generalizations). You do not need to draw conclusions that stand test in a court of law. Instead your aim is to open up some new possibilities. Or to add a new dimension, or simply a new specific idea about values, to our already large stock of values, without implying that you have the whole story. Or to make some suggestions about how the circle of ethical concern is expanding, for you, or for others, or deepening in ways we perhaps have not yet noticed. Discoveries are *beginnings*.

3. Temper your conclusions with some reflections about the limits of your discovery or experience. Consider what it is about yourself (your background, your values, your lifestyle and dominant concerns) that may have made your discovery or experience possible.

Another way to ask this question is: how might you understand someone else who did not have the same experience you did? What factors may close off such experiences for some people, or transform the experience into something else? Or again, are there other possible interpretations of the same experience? For example, Walker's reaction to the crisis in Blue's life was to stop eating meat. You might react quite differently: by trying to help Blue himself, for instance. Why do you think Walker changed in the way she did? Under what conditions might you or someone else change in a different way—or perhaps not change at all? If people's experience is likely to be similar, what follows from that fact? If people's experience is likely to be different, what follows from *that* fact?

There is much more to say about these things, more than any short discussion such as this one can say. Again, though, if your teacher expects you to write in this style in your paper, your assigned readings should offer you some models to follow. Read the full version of Walker's "Am I Blue?." In fact, read the whole collection: Walker's essays are often models of intensely personal and critical ethical engagement in a discovery style. Another well-known essay you might examine is

Philip Hallie, "From Cruelty to Goodness," which is the first essay in the Sommers collection already cited. Hallie's is a scholar's story, the story of a search for (and discovery of) goodness in the midst of evil, in his case the Nazi holocaust. You might take it as a model of a discovery paper that goes beyond personal experience to a research project as well.

Discovery papers in ethics may use a much wider variety of styles than argument papers: people and their experiences are both very different. Many approaches to writing are appropriate, from the simplest personal narratives to diary entries or poetry. Read enough of Natalie Goldberg's *Writing Down the Bones* (Shambhala Publications, 1986) to get some inspiration and some good advice.

The argument style and the discovery style hardly exhaust the options in ethics. They are only two of many common styles at present. Other styles are also possible: dialogues, for example; parables and sermons; stories; purely factual or journalistic accounts; "confessions"; and so on. Your job in finding an ethical voice is partly to find (or create) the style or styles that work best for you.

Students may also wish to consult *A 21st Century Ethical Toolbox*, Chapter 13, for an approach more explicit about the various goals of an ethical paper than I can be here.

Finally, whatever style and whatever topic and approach you choose, I trust that as you plan and write your paper you will not forget all of the other advice you are offered in this book. Avoid mere appeals to authority. Try to think creatively about the options and alternatives in an ethically problematic situation. Integrate values rather than polarizing them. Keep an open heart and an open mind. Take your time—and give yourself the time to take.